A Book of Life

Ron Stegman

VITALITY

buzz, bliss + books

To Michele,

Our daughters, Kira and Shana,

Our friends,

And my former students

In gratitude
to the VATRONS
who breathed life into this volume
by pre-ordering their copy

Ron's Men's Group who has been meeting Mondays for years...listed here with their wives...
Dave & Mary Koenig-Clapp, Jim & Pam Jurgens, Bob & Star Mierenfeld,
Vern & Marilyn Petry, Ron & Michele Stegman

and these friends...

Gary Adams, Jerry Ahluwalia, Susan Alberi, Mike Arnold, Adam Aunspaw, Ron Beerman, John Beiting, George Beluan, John Bender, John Bennet, Mary R Bernard, Tim Bessler, Harry Blanton, Russ Blessing, Helen M Buswinka, Michael Charrier, Jacqueline Charrier, Alexander Childs, Joe Collins, Katie Collins, Peter Corrigan, Steve Cox, Shannon Cox, Connie Deardorff, Jennifer Donahue & the St. Xavier Library, James W Downie, John Emmett, Denver England, Stephanie Epperson, Dan & Marcia Erdman, Damien Eversmann, Dennis Federle, Alex Fischer, Jean Foutch, Doug Franz, Jennie Freda, Anne Frick, Jeremy Fulwiler, Linda Gloeckler, Cori Grandle, Andrew Guinigundo, Keith Hafer, Brady Hall, Robert Harting, Hayley Hatfield, Robin Heberling, Eric Heis, Linda J Hendley, Brett Hennie, Diane Herrmann, Tess Hudepohl, RuthAnn Hyland Henderson, Roberta Jackson, Matt Johnston, Matt & Rachel Kemper, Donna Kimball, Matthew Klooster, Patrick Klus, Richard Klus, Mary Lou Kohne, Mary F Korb, William Krider, Linda Lacunza, Joseph Langley, Linda Legeza, Jeffrey Loos, Michael H Marchal, Susan McGarvey, Therese McNulty, Quen Metzler, John Meyer, Sherry Miller, Zak Morgan, James Muenchen, Patrick Mulvaney, Cindy Mulvaney, Lisa Myers, Stephanie Nelson, Eric Nichols, Peg Niehaus, Mike North, William Oconnell, David Ott, Belinda Paisley, Angie Paolo, Lora Pateras, Mark Patterson, Joyce Pauly, Sandi Petrou, Mary Plummer, Linda Preminger, Martha P Rajandran, Andy Rauen, Janet Reder, Brent Reiner, Melissa Rettig, Frederick Reuter & Judy Wimberg, Karen Reynolds, Gary Robbins, Eric Robbins, John F Robbins, Martin Roberts, Michael Rosal, Thomas Rowe, Douglas Rush, Gary Sabourin, Chad Sandhas, William Sandquist, Mary Schewe, Judy Schrand, Stephen Schrantz, Jennifer Schulkers, Liz Sedler, Diane Seifert, Timothy Shafer, Brian Shircliff, Gregory Shumavon, Marilyn Sick, Matthew Siemer, Geralyn Sparough, David Specht, Jay Stahl, Steven Stegman, Ed Stegman, Carole Stegman, Joseph Stolz, Doug Storer, Eileen Strauchler, Bruce Strickland, Rob Strub, Bridget Tanner, Lynn Tarvin Sparks, Rich Tatgenhorst, Ashley Thomas, Jim Tomaszewski, Marcia Tuznik, Gary Vaughn, Joyce Wade, Samuel Watts, Katie Weaver, Larry Weber, Joseph Wells, Brendan Welsh, Tuck Whitehurst, Mark Wilkins, John Williams, Rhonda Wilson, Paul Wilson, Michael Wilson, Stephen Winhusen, James Wolf, Stacey Woolley, Michele Zins, Linda Zinsmeister Hendley, John Zuehlke

CONTENTS

introduction

Over 50 years ago this book began to take shape as I realized that many of the stories people shared with me were full of life and meaning. I started writing down some of these stories and using them in my teaching. I realized the best way to connect with students was through sharing our experiences – from those I had gathered as well as listening to the students themselves. This made such a profound impact on me, my teaching, and the students' experience, that I started thinking these stories could help others as well.

We all have stories within us. Everyone. We are a story! As I collected stories, I thought someday I would have a little book of these events and experiences. We all have questions about life, about being human, about creation, about finding meaning. I thought if I had a variety of stories, it would help people to be aware of life, to feel life, to appreciate life, to have reverence for life. We all take so much for granted. So much is lost in our daily living that could be seen and felt more deeply. I feel that anyone could do what I'm doing now by truly paying attention to what others are telling them and recording their words. My hope is that the people who read my book will take that up in some way in their own life.

There are different themes that appear throughout the book. There is simplicity and the beauty of creation. There is also suffering and loss. These, too, are a part of us and shape our lives. Some stories may impact one person and not another. Some may not affect you at one point in your life but will affect you deeply at another time. I find that each time I read through the stories I've collected, they will touch me in a different way. We all relate to different experiences depending on what our own experiences have been.

There are quite a few stories about animals, which I think move us emotionally and speak to us about nature and being present in life. Animals have a simplicity and beauty about their acceptance of life just as it is. I think most human beings respond to animals in a profound way as they teach us how to feel alive and be in the moment. Nature gives us peace and quiet and helps us go to our inner self and to our creator. This can help us love more deeply and have more reverence and appreciation for the world surrounding us. Hopefully these stories help you to see the goodness of these creatures as well as how important all life is.

As this collection developed, I felt that I wanted to listen to more and more people so I could show the entire depth of what others have gone through in life. It was frustrating because I could not cover every topic. Gathering these stories for so many years, I have collected a wide range of experiences. But even in a whole lifetime you cannot hear every person's story. Even so, I hope anyone who picks up this book can find a piece of themselves in some aspects of it. Hopefully, the stories awaken much of life in you. Everything in this book is true. Only some names and small details are changed to protect people.

I set out to write this book with the idea of reaching everyone. I wish every single person could read and connect with it because we are all in this life together. We are all human beings even though we are all different. I don't mean for this book to preach to anyone on how to live. But I do want everyone to be able to look at these stories and say, "I can relate to this life. I can feel a connection to another person telling what they have gone through." I want you to find an appreciation for creation, others, and yourself. I want you to think about your own life and experiences, your struggles and gifts. I want someone who doesn't live like me to still be able to relate in some way. I don't want anyone to be left out. I hope to give everyone's life a little more meaning and let their search for meaning go deeper, like the stories did for me.

I believe questions help people to reflect more deeply. When I was teaching, I found they would stir things up and really get the students thinking. So, along with these stories, there are questions to help you think more about life. If those I have suggested don't resonate with you, they can be used as a guide. Ask yourself how the story moves you and develop your own questions.

Faith, religion, and God come up in most people's lives, so you will hear that mentioned often throughout this book. However, this is not presented to push a certain religion or belief, but just to allow each storyteller to share their own journey. This can help all of us to reflect on our personal journey and how we formed our unique view of life. Whether with a god or without a god, we can all reflect on and embrace our personal version of faith, spirituality, creation, and connection. No matter what our own beliefs are, it is important to listen to and think about the experiences of others. These stories were gathered from different people from all walks of life and their experience in the world.

I want people to use this book as a chance to reflect on the meaning of life, especially in relation to love, reverence, and relationships. What does this experience of living mean to us and to those whose stories we are reading? How can we find meaning in our own lives through this opportunity to read the words of others?

The narrative that runs through the entire book and connects the stories is that of my wife, Michele, and I building our log house. It was such a powerful experience that I felt it became a foundational part of my history of storytelling and integral to the book. Anyone can build a house, but this one has an unusual history where incredible events happened. Most of the house was built from recycled materials, helping us to build it debt free, and giving us freedom to live a simple life. Thousands of people have visited our home, experienced retreats, joined in celebrations, immersed themselves in nature, and shared their stories here. This house holds an incredible story of life within its walls. These pages about our house represent persistence, building life and community, freedom, and finding gifts in simplicity.

The art in this book was all done by family members. The art may speak to some as a story as well. When I began, I thought I would do this book by myself. Instead, it became a family project with everyone helping in some way. I found that you need help in whatever you do. My family really jumped in and helped with storytelling, advice, editing, and telling their own stories. It became wonderful to share this book with them. They became so engaged that this has become a story in itself.

As I heard these stories over the years, they would make me pause and think about how I'm living, how others are living, and make me appreciate the gifts of life. I would read them over and have those feelings again and again. At certain points in my life, I would find they affected me more deeply than other times. Yet they were always with me and always touched me. I especially appreciated when they would stir emotion in me. As I collected the pieces for this book, I found I would pause and reflect more about what was happening around me. Someone would be talking and suddenly I would hear them say something that moved me. I would say, "Wait, I want to write that down," and then it would stay with me. I began to question things more deeply because I was always looking for the story in it. What is this saying? What story is here? How can this be shared? All of these stories have shaped my life for many years, and now I'm finally able to share some of the best of them with the world.

1

MICHELE: The first time I saw Ron was at Westwood Town Hall. I had joined a theatre group even though at the time I was a rather shy introvert. When I walked in, there was music playing and some of the people were dancing. That's when I saw Ron. He was dressed in baggy clothes and not dancing very well, but his eyes were sparkling. He was smiling and enjoying himself so much all eyes were on him, including mine. I couldn't look away. When we talked, he was so excited to show me his **Book of Life**, enthusiastically showing me page after page of photos and anecdotes he had collected. He was so full of life himself, filling everyone around him with the same joy he had. I knew right then, this is the man I wanted to marry. However, it took a couple of years and a trick to get him to ask me out.

I did everything to get his attention. He was always nice to me, but he was more interested in the lively dancers than someone quiet. Every time I went to the town hall, I looked for Ron. One day, he was there rehearsing a play but saw me and came out to talk. He had recently returned from a trip to Greece and I mentioned that I had been taking a class in New Testament Greek. He was impressed with that, and I thought, If I can get him to my house for some reason, he'll feel obligated to ask me out. He was really excited about his Greek trip so I said, "I would love to see your slides! Want to bring them over to my house and show me?" Of course he wanted to do that, and I thought, Finally! He came to the house, showed me his slides, and as he was getting ready to leave, he was

standing there at the door looking uncomfortable, fiddling with his keys, and I thought, He's going to ask me out but he doesn't want to. He feels obligated to do it, but I'm going to say yes. I could tell it was with reluctance that he asked me out for the next weekend, but I said yes.

RON: When I came back for our date, I still remember exactly what Michele was wearing when she opened the door. When I saw her standing there looking so beautiful and natural, that was when I fell in love with her. That was the beginning.

MICHELE: We dated, and saw each other almost every night. Every day as I taught school, I thought about him all day and could hardly wait for him to arrive each evening. Thirteen months later we got married.

Forbes' Silk Moth, Roy King

The Delivery

As we prepared for the delivery of our first baby, my wife had decided to have a natural birth. So here we were in this prep room for delivery. I stood next to the monitor of the heartbeat and contractions. I would read the monitor and tell her, "A contraction is now building! Now it's at the top! Now it's going away!" I wanted to help, and this felt like all I could do. She yelled, "I know what's happening!"

She finally said, "I want something to ease the pain." But the doctor replied, "Not now, you are ready to deliver."

As we entered the delivery room the nurse told me to put a mask on my face. I did so. When the doctor entered, he said, "Take off the mask! The first thing the baby should see is your face." I took it off. He left for a few minutes and the nurse told me, "Put that mask on!" So, I did. When the doctor reentered, he told me to take the mask off, so I did once again.

The doctor then said my wife was ready to begin pushing. I looked on with disbelief as I saw a circle of matted dark hair appear. At this point I was thinking the baby looked like it would have a cigar shaped head. I was worried that the baby would have a physical problem. I was ready to catch the baby when, suddenly, my wife pushed hard, and the baby came flying out and landed on the bed. The doctor said, "It's a girl!"

The new baby girl looked around as if to say, "What happened?" Not a cry, simply a look. They placed her in my wife's arms. She seemed very calm and at peace.

I was in disbelief as my wife had pushed so hard she had tearing and had to be taken for minor surgery. I wondered how she was so calm with all this blood pouring out.

The nurse took the new little girl and placed a cap on her head. They would be out of the room for a while, so she put this newborn daughter into my arms. As they left the room and I held her, I thought, "This is the rest of my life – to care for her." I felt like I was floating for days.

— Ron Stegman

Birth is wonderful and messy. What does this say to me about life?

Why are we so awed by birth? What does new life teach me?

Love Heals

The day was warm, springtime, and I was walking past the home of a friend when she called me over and, smiling, said, "Look what I have here." On a blanket spread out on the fresh grass was a small boy. As they had adopted children, I replied, "How wonderful. Did you just adopt him?"

"We hope to finish the process soon, but for now we can keep him. How old do you think he is?"

Looking at the small boy I noticed that he made no sound, nor did he move. "I would say three years old."

She answered, "No, he is six years old, but cannot talk, cannot walk, cannot feed himself, nor has he been toilet trained. He was abandoned at a very young age and was in a home for abandoned babies and young children. The home was extremely busy with many children and, as he was no trouble and never cried, the staff would allow him to remain in the crib to never have to deal with him. He was quiet and seemed to accept everything.

Basically, they would feed him and that was all. No one talked with him nor was he taught many things. Eventually, he became indifferent to life and surroundings. He has not bothered to walk, feed himself, nor even move."

I could see his physical development had been stunted and he did appear to be much younger. She smiled and told me the family would love him back to health. I wondered whether it could be done.

Six months passed and I visited her home again. I walked into the kitchen and sitting in a highchair was a very pudgy boy with food smeared around his face and down his front. His legs were swinging, and his arms and hands were busily tapping spoons and trays. This motor machine laughed, yelled in happiness, and he spoke single words such as, "Food, Mom." This was the same child I had seen six months earlier.

His mother, smiling proudly, said, "He's a very active child now, happy, and the family loves him."

— Ron Stegman (written when he was 19)

The love healed! How has my love helped someone else to heal?

How do I feel love plays into the meaning of life?

Have I felt unloved in my life? What did I do?

The Gift

I was 14 the year my mother died. During the mid-1950s, cancer was rarely discussed in anything other than hushed tones, and never around children. As a result, I was unprepared for her death, which affected me greatly. My father was a very stoic man who seldom showed his emotions. Nevertheless, he did his best to comfort me while he also mourned in silence.

We lived on a farm on a quiet country road to which we had moved when I was five. My parents had always wanted a home with enough land to plant a big garden, raise a few chickens and perhaps, eventually buy a cow for milk.

Our nearest neighbors, who lived across a field and on the other side of the creek, had farmed their land for many years before we moved in next door. They had dairy cows, pigs, chickens, and always planted a huge garden. They had five children, the three youngest being within four years of my age. The closest to me in age was Joyce and, since there were very few children in the area, and since we were in the same grade at school, we quickly became friends.

Ours was an idyllic childhood, playing in the woods and beside the creek, taking picnic lunches that our mothers prepared for us to eat under a big old oak tree at the top of the hill behind our barn, climbing the ladder to the hayloft in the barn to share little girls' secrets and little girls' dreams, and sometimes going up to the pasture on their hill with Joyce's two older brothers to drive the cows home to be milked in the late afternoon.

After my mother's death, my father and I coped as best we could; however, nothing was ever the same.

On the morning of my fifteenth birthday, two weeks before Christmas, and less than two months after my mother's death, my father and I were having breakfast before leaving for the day. I had to go to school and my father had to head out for work, but then there was an unexpected knock at the door. When I went to open it, I saw Joyce standing on the porch.

She was holding a cardboard box. In the background, I could see her mother's car, idling in the driveway.

"Happy birthday. Mom wanted you to have this," she said, handing me the box.

After thanking her, I took the box to the kitchen to open it. Inside the box was a cake that her mother had baked for me. Her mom was a busy farm wife who had three children still at home and a full-time job. Yet, she had found the time in her hectic week to bake a birthday cake for me, because she was afraid that I would not get one that year.

It was on that cold, dark winter morning that I learned a valuable lesson. Sometimes the best gifts do not come from a department store, wrapped in colorful paper and bound with bright ribbons. Sometimes the best gift is a simple one like a homemade from scratch, two-layer yellow cake, covered with butter cream frosting and presented in a simple cardboard box, given by someone with a kind and loving heart.

— Sue Rheinfrank

A kind act of love can stay with us for a lifetime. Can I think of one that was given to me?

How have I shown love to someone who needed help?

Do I treasure simple gifts that I have been given?

Your Generous Love

I have always appreciated your love for me and your firm commitment to me. I never doubt these two wonderful gifts. I have felt comfortable and relaxed because of your love. Your commitment to me makes me love you more.

I always see you working at this love and this commitment. These qualities are so very evident, and I believe these have greatly enhanced our marriage. I believe that if you thought my best development would be for me to leave, you would want me to go as you are so concerned for my happiness.

You have been such a wonderful gift to me that much peace has flowed into my life.

I do hope that I never disappoint your generous love. You have taught me so much about love. I have often thought of the time you tried to protect me from lightning in our first week of marriage. I remember you, half asleep, moving next to me in bed, covering my body with yours, to protect me from a storm and lightening outside. Then and there you showed your care for me. I believe that act meant more than the wedding vows. That was a physical expression of the vows. Even now you tell me how I am the center of your life.

So, thank you for trusting your life to me. What an honor. A beautiful gift you give to me. Thank you for putting your life into my care. You live out the scripture words, "Where you go, so will I go." I am so blessed. I love you.

— Ron, written to Michele

Have I experienced such pure love in my life?

Love is demanding and takes commitment but gives joy and happiness to both. Am I willing to do this with those in my life?

What is the most difficult commitment for me to make?

Our Special Chicken

For six years my partner and I ran a bed and breakfast on a ranch in Jackson, Wyoming. We had ponies, pigs, goats, a sheep, and several chickens. Often, people would call us to see if we could take in an unwanted farm animal. We would most likely always say yes! The ranch was a bit like a retirement community for these animals.

One day I got a call from a woman saying she had to move quickly from her house, but she had 20 chickens and 6 ducks that needed a home. We hopped right in the truck and drove to visit her farm. When we arrived, we soon became aware that the animals were treated poorly. We knew we didn't need 26 more birds, but we didn't hesitate to load them all up to take with us. Most of the birds were dirty, starving, and neglected. The woman told me she was having a hard time but did indeed love her chickens and ducks. Despite their appearance, I believed her. She mentioned one chicken in particular that was hard for her to let go of, but she had no choice. Her name was Helen, and she was mostly blind. I reassured her we would take good care of them all, especially Helen.

When we arrived home, we opened the back of the truck and let the birds wander freely around the property. They quickly seemed to realize they were now in a safe environment. They introduced themselves to the other animals and made themselves quite comfortable in our hen house cuddled up with the other chickens.

All except Helen. Being mostly blind she was totally lost within her new surroundings. She stayed by my side and on my lap. We made her a special area in the barn where she could feel safe, and we guided her to her water and food bowl. She was so intelligent and was able to navigate her space very well once we gave her some direction. At first, she would follow us around the ranch all the time, but each day that went by, she became more confident to explore a bit further.

Her favorite thing continued to be sitting on laps and having a chat. It was as if she wanted to tell us all about her life and adventures. I started playing her music with my guitar and she would settle down, making little chicken "purrs," while her eyes would close. If I would pause, she would use her beak to pluck the strings on the guitar to get me going again.

Eventually, Helen had her own bunch of chickens that preferred to follow her around due to her kind and gentle nature. Now she was the leader instead of the follower. She was really flourishing! When she had first come to us, I saw her as a totally defenseless chicken, but she proved to be independent, graceful, and beautiful.

One spring, one of our other hens had a brood of chicks, but decided one of the chicks was not well enough to keep and kicked it out of the nest. I decided to put it on Helen's side of the barn, and, without hesitation, Helen literally took the chick under her wing. She started showing it how to navigate its surroundings like she once had to learn. She kept it warm and safe from other chickens and raised it as her own. The beauty of nature, survival, and the circle of life shined through Helen's actions. Once a little chick I had been concerned wouldn't be able to survive on her own, she was now teaching others to thrive.

— Shana Stegman

Love begets love. Where have I experienced love that helped me to love more generously?

Life is made better by such acts as described here. Where has my life been made better from a particular situation or event?

What creatures have taught me to be gentle or considerate? What did they do?

Sight and Touch

I went to the Southside today to do a house repair. I went into a house where you could see through the boards of the house. They had dirt floors and no electricity. There were many children, and the wife was pregnant. There was one little boy, seven or eight years old, who was blind. I asked him if he wanted to touch me to know me and he shook his head yes. He touched my arm and face, very gently.

— Carole Stegman

How do I approach others so they can see and experience things in the way that works best for them?

What does it mean to connect to another person in this way and give them understanding?

The Alzheimer's Unit

Today my wife and I visited my mother-in-law who is in an Alzheimer's care unit. She sits in a wheelchair with her head bent over to the right, no movement, and her eyes stare into nowhere. My wife came to her and, looking into her eyes, said, "I am your daughter." Her mother seemed to understand in some way that this person was someone special and she began to softly cry. Then she returned to her inner world, whatever that may be.

The surroundings were sad and mostly aged women, sitting in their chairs or wheelchairs eating pureed food. For the most part, they ate silently with a little spoon. A few spoke to one another. One appeared to sleep as she was offered food and her mouth moved often. Her eyes never opened, nor did she move her body. Some walked about saying words which made little sense or were not connected with reality.

My wife began feeding her mother with the teaspoon and her mother would open her lips to take the food, her eyes, for the most part, in a blank stare. Every so often she would utter some incoherent words or sounds. A few times she used actual words. Once she smiled. Then I had the opportunity to feed her some of the meal. She ate everything. An older man, named Ramon, who did not have Alzheimer's but took his meals with them, sat across the table and had no trouble eating and conversing.

The experience was almost surreal and often sad. We wondered what her mother was thinking. Is she thinking? When she mumbled words and sounds which made no sense was she speaking thoughts? Does she have joy? Is she sad? Is she aware of her surroundings? What is going on inside her? Why do humans come to this type of life stage? I thought, this could be myself or my wife in a few years. Being in the surroundings reminded me of our own vulnerable life. All of this was stressful and reflective at the same time.

As we prepared to leave, the man, Ramon, who had sat across the dinner table, said to us, "When you fed her, you fed me." Perhaps this was our answer to all the questions that came up for us during this day. I felt that I heard God's words in this moment, and it gave me a thrill of meaning. He knew that what you do to one person helps others. He saw this act of love from us and felt the love within himself. Someone caring for her means he is also not forgotten. Humanity is all connected, and he grasped that in this simple act.

— Ron Stegman

Is Ramon giving me some answer to soothing the suffering of others?

The human condition is often difficult. What do I feel as I read this description of these surroundings?

We need one another. How do I see good in experiences of human struggles?

At the Zoo

I worked as an educator at the zoo where I would teach the public about animals. I would bring out various animals they could interact with and touch. One afternoon, I was out teaching people about a corn snake. A girl in her late teens walked up to me with her parents. The parents told her, "This girl has a snake that you can touch." The parents placed her hand on the snake, and she rubbed her hand gently along the scales. Her face lit up and she kept saying, "Holy moley, holy moley." Her parents described each thing about the snake to her. She was blind, and she finally had a chance to see something at the Zoo for herself through touching the snake.

— Kira King

Do I appreciate how important touch is to humans and creatures?

What aspects of life am I "blind" to? How can I experience these things in my own way?

How can I be a light to others?

The Rug

I look at our living room rug and this 35-year-old Oriental rug speaks to me about life. Twenty-five years earlier I played "Alligator" on this rug with my two small daughters. In the game, I would stand in the middle of the rug, which was the swamp for my monster alligator. Then my two little daughters would attempt to run over to the other side without me catching one of them. When I did catch one, there would be laughter and yells of surprise and delight. Then that daughter would be the alligator. This became one of our favorite games. Twenty-five years later, as I look at this rug, that wonderful time with my daughters returns. The rug holds the treasures of life within it. I wish we could play Alligator again.

— Ron Stegman

What items in my life are special to me for what they represent?

Can I still feel happy times from childhood? What were they?

As an adult, have I kept the spirit of play or have I lost that playfulness?

The Shooting Stars

As my future wife and I stood in the darkness on a high hill overlooking the lighted city, we could see the multitude of stars above. This was the time. I reached into my jacket and pulled out the engagement ring to place on her finger. Just as I placed the ring, a shooting star raced across from East to West over the city. Only a few seconds, but a wonder and a symbol for us.

Some 40 years later, on a clear night, my daughter and her future husband stood looking at the stars with their feet in the shallow waters of the Caribbean. He knew this was the time. He had no ring, but he turned and asked her to marry him. After she accepted, she thought of our experience and looked up at the sky with her new fiancé. Suddenly, a shooting star raced across the sky, lighting up the night.

— Ron Stegman

Have I been awed by a particular event in my life?

Does life itself speak to me of wonder?

My Lost Friend

When I was seven, my little neighbor friend and I planned to go swimming at the local pool in the afternoon. I went to his house and called for him to come out. But his mother appeared at the door. I asked for Bobby. With almost no expression on her face, or so it seemed to me, she said that her child had left earlier with some older boys and instead of the pool they had gone to the river. And then she told me he had drowned in that river. For a moment I froze. I could only see her face and hear her strange words. She said nothing else, and I left not really understanding what had happened. However, over these many years, the thought of him and his sudden loss has stayed with me. Every so often I suddenly think of him and grieve the loss. I believe that single event has influenced my entire life. When his memory comes to me, I think about how he didn't get to live. It reminds me that life is precarious and to appreciate the gift of my own life. His was so short. It made me realize, as a young child, that we all die. In all these years, this hits me with the experience of life and death.

— Ron Stegman

Have I had an experience where life seemed to stand still that has stayed with me always?

As a child he did not understand fully what had happened. How does one process events like this as we grow to understanding? How have experiences like this influenced me

2

MICHELE: After we were married, we moved into an apartment together. I felt so confined in that little apartment. I kept leaving the front door open wide just to be able to breathe. Ron was a city boy, but he loved being in nature, taking walks in a nearby park, and being outside. He said he wanted to stay in an apartment and have a place in the country, but I said, "If your heart is in nature, in the country, why should we stay all week in town? Let's build a house in the country and live there."

RON: While we were in that apartment we wanted to travel — a lot. I was interested in the Third World, the poor. She was interested in learning more about the culture of other countries. For our honeymoon, we went to Greece. I wanted to show her those slides again but in person! Then we went to India. We stayed for two months, traveling from New Delhi to Kathmandu, from Srinagar to the Taj Mahal. We saw beauty and beggars, the rich and the very poor sleeping and living on the streets. That trip impacted both our lives.

When we came back from India, we wanted to live more simply to identify with the poor of the world. One way I wanted to identify with them was by eating less meat as that was something they did not have much of.

MICHELE: I didn't know how to cook vegetarian, but I learned.

MICHELE: I had always wanted to live on a farm in the country because when I was little, we lived on a farm with my grandmother, and I was so happy there. All my cousins, the whole family, would visit there all the time. There were always cousins to play with, food from the garden, and the barn and creek to explore. We moved away when I was six, but we visited my grandmother's all the time. I loved being there and I thought, This is what I want. I want a home in the country. I want a farm and I want it to be a place for people to come. That's what I told Ron. I kept saying, "I really want to move to the country."

RON: So, we wanted a house and land in the country, we wanted to live simply, and neither of us wanted to go into debt. How could we do this with no debt?

MICHELE: We also wanted our house to be unique. We wanted something different from the typical houses you see up and down the street. Even more importantly, we wanted a place where people would visit and want to come back. A special place that made people feel good and reflected who we are as people. We decided the best way to go about this would be to buy land and build our own home.

We would see ads in the paper for land, look at the places, get home and call to put in an offer. "Oh, we just sold it." Time after time.

RON: Every. Time. So, we prayed. We prayed for a piece of land that was beautiful, not on a main road, and was something we could afford.

Right after that, I bought a Cincinnati *Enquirer*. There was a small ad for land — 20 acres in Guilford, Indiana. Feeling hopeful, we called, and he said, "Yes, it's still available," and told us how to get there. We drove out immediately.

MICHELE: I was so afraid we would be disappointed again. We took money to put down on it, because if we liked it, we were going to buy it right then. We were not going to let another piece of property get away from us.

RON: We met the guy and walked through the 20 acres of fields and woods.

MICHELE: The land was back on a long, gravel road. It was isolated, with a narrow road up to the top of the hill, over a creek and through tall, dense woods. There was a field at the top of the hill which would be a perfect spot for a house. And there were more woods beyond that field. We felt at peace there. And joyous, free. It wasn't ours yet, but we had saved enough to buy it.

RON: We said, "This is it!" We asked him, "How much?" and he said, "Eight thousand dollars."

MICHELE: Ever one to bargain, I asked, "How much will you sell it to us for if we pay cash?" Oh, his eyes lit up! He said, "Seventy-five hundred." We gave him the money we had brought, then came back a couple of days later with a check for the rest. He gave us the deed, and we recorded it. We had land! Later on, we also bought an adjoining 26 acres.

RON: Now we had 20 acres — cheap — in an area we knew nothing about. We had no debt, but no house. Now the question became, how are we going to get a house without debt? We looked at A-frames, new log home kits...

MICHELE: We looked at teepees, yurts. We looked at everything, just as long as it was different.

RON: We even thought about a stone house, but it would take two years to build what we wanted. And they were all around $50,000 and we thought, We'd have debt. How do we get a house with no debt?

We had been sharing our frustrations with people around us and, finally, the son of a fellow teacher told us, "There's a guy selling an old, pioneer-built log cabin that he dismantled. It's on a flatbed truck, but it could be reassembled." So, we called and asked if we could see the logs.

MICHELE: We had decided that a log cabin would work for us, but an old log cabin? Even better! I was excited about the idea of living in a pioneer-built home. We went to look at it. At first sight, my heart kind of sank. The cabin was supposed to be 40 feet by 20 feet, so the logs barely fit on that 40-foot flatbed truck, but the pile of logs didn't look big enough to build a whole house. And they looked terrible.

This cabin had been built in the mid-1840's and had been lived in until two weeks before it was dismantled. The man had just taken it down. The owners had covered the exterior of the house with clapboard and there were still pieces of it clinging here and there. They had plastered and wallpapered the inside and lots of that plaster and wallpaper was still there. The openings between the logs had been stuffed with rocks and mud and whatever those original pioneers could find. There was a lot of that left on the logs, too.

He had a picture of the house with a chart and had numbered the logs. He said, "This is how it goes back together." We were skeptical. We worried that these dirt-covered logs wouldn't actually make a house. I guess he saw our hesitancy and reduced the price from $4,000 to $3,500.

RON: We said we'd take them. I was to meet him the next day to pay him. But, that evening, we started thinking about how much easier it might be to just buy a new log house kit. We knew nothing about building with these old logs and got nervous about it. I told Michele, "I'll go and tell him no."

MICHELE: I said, "Just call him." He said, "No, I think I should tell him in person."

RON: I drove out and told him, "I don't think we want them." And he said, "Why? I guarantee they're all okay. All the logs are there. If there's anything missing, I will replace it with new logs." I thought, Well why not? You know, risk it! They're not that bad. Why not! So, I said, "I'll take them." Then I came back to Michele, hopeful that she would not be too mad that I had made this decision to buy them on my own after we had agreed not to.

MICHELE: As soon as Ron left, I started feeling sad. I was wishing we had decided to take the risk to build with those logs. But, in 1973, there was no way to contact him. When Ron came back, he seemed a little hesitant. He finally smiled and said, "I bought the logs." I jumped up and hugged him. I said, "As soon as you left, I thought about it more and changed my mind. I want to do this! I'm so glad!" I think he was just a little relieved!

Ron Stegman

Botanical Bear, Roy King

Words of a Monk

One day an older Trappist monk shared the following reflections with a group at his monastery:

In our society we are always measuring ourselves against others. When the love of God is not developed in us, then we look for it in others. The hunger for love is infinite. When the love of God is developed, then you can love others. The human heart is made for God. Whatever the parent was, they gave us life. And thus, we are for eternity. We live forever. There is no way to grasp this.

Life is shaky. How are you going to cope without the faith? It is hard enough with the faith. We never give up. We keep coming back. Our parents also gave us the faith. We are also united with them at another level. When you have God then life is meaningful, beautiful.

— Ron Stegman

Am I a hopeful person? What do I believe I am made for?

Do I have a restless heart? Do I see myself as good?

A Magical Moment

During the holiday season the zoo has a special event called Festival of Lights. There are thousands and thousands of Christmas lights throughout the park. They decorate trees, plants, and the grounds. An especially beautiful place is the lake located in the center of the zoo. The various colored lights surround the lake on trees, bushes, and plants. There is a large Christmas tree that stands in the middle of the lake on a small island. This tree has many lights, which change with the music.

On a visit to the Festival of Lights in the early evening, I witnessed the antics of kea birds who entertained us. I also saw a screech owl up close and a large owl who kept calling to me. These alone were a gift to behold.

The evening became even more remarkable when I stood at the lake. The music of Pachelbel's Canon was playing and the lights surrounding the lake were changing colors according to the music. The entire scene and atmosphere were almost magical. There were waterfowl swimming in the lake – a variety of ducks, geese, and swans. They would occasionally give a call but, for the most part, they glided silently through the water with the colored light reflecting off them.

Suddenly, with the music, the lights, with my arm around Michele, and the reflections on the lake, the moment took me beyond myself. Briefly I felt as if I were one with these birds, with creation. It was almost as if I were outside my body. This all was very brief, but so exhilarating and joyful. I did not want this to end. Is this experience a mirror of what eternity could be like for me?

— Ron Stegman

Recall a special moment in life. What was it and where was I?

Have I experienced love that changed me?

Have I had feelings so intense that life became different for me afterward? What happened?

Reflections on Belief

This is one father's reflection to his daughter, who is an atheist. She asked him why he believed in God, and this was his response to her:

St. Augustine wrote, "Our hearts are restless until they rest in God." This is part of the sadness of many and you. We experience sadness, frustration in death, constant change, loss. People want this constant changing and loss to go away and there to be a permanent world. Only one source is permanent. Our hearts yearn for fulfillment and peace and will only find this in Our Source, which is already in us.

Faith takes a step into trust – a leap. But faith is not blind. It is based on our experiences, intuition, insights, desires within us, history of people, the reasons people want more, a God experience, and the subconscious. Finally, we take a leap. All life is based on faith and trust.

Jesus said, "Ask and you will receive," "seek and you will find." Jesus is saying your hearts will be answered in your faith leap and journey. When people do this, life changes. Their eyes are opened even though there are questions. Some do and some do not as we see in the Gospels.

You will never have true peace and joy until you find meaning and I think the ultimate reality is The Source. Most people's faith is childlike and that serves them. But deep faith is an openness to growth and to questions and taking the step into faith in God as they understand God.

This is still mystery, but also wonder. I have questions and doubts but faith in this mystery of God.

— Ron Stegman

What helps me to believe there is more than we experience?

No matter if we are spiritual or an atheist, we all look for meaning in life. Where do I find meaning?

I Want My Comfort Zone

On a student mission trip to the interior of Mexico, I met with the students early in the trip. The temperature was near 100 and unrelenting. Most said they wanted to go home. They spoke of their frustration with trying to understand the language, the people looking at them, the very poor conditions, missing their own homes. They were bring pushed out of their comfort zone.

After a time talking together, they seemed better, but still wanted to leave. At that point, there was a knock at the door and a group of women from the community came in. They told us that they had come to welcome us and they began to sing songs for us. The students joined in when they could. The women invited us all to lunch and left. I turned to the students and said, "And you thought you were not welcome here." This changed everything for them.

That evening we met with the families the students were staying with. The families told them, "You are our family now." A very old lady gave them each a personal response to their names and said they were her grandchildren.

This was a hard place to be, yet a good place to be. At the end of the trip, one student said, "This experience has felt like 19 years and not 19 days because of all I have gained" They had many years' worth of life and learning in a short time.

— Ron Stegman

Perhaps when I am uncomfortable, I grow as a person the most. Do I have examples of this in my life?

What have I learned during times of change or pain?

What surprising event in my life helped me to accept challenges that I faced?

Philip Neri

There was a man in the 15th century who inspires me to live now with joy. Many have not heard of this inspiring, simple man, yet he influenced many in the city of Rome. His name was Philip Neri.

He believed in laughter, especially when people around him became too serious. He walked with a joyful spirit and even acted as a clown as he walked the streets of Rome.

He saw animals as innocent creatures and celebrated our humanity. He lived from the heart and spoke from the heart. People sought him out, for his presence gave people hope, healing, and forgiveness. He urged those around him to sing, to be humble, to enjoy the simple things of life. Those around him felt called to be better, to love, to celebrate life.

He knew men and women could cause pain, could deceive, could do evil, but he remained cheerful and challenged them to let go of those things which hurt others and themselves. If someone tried to fool or hurt him, he saw through it, but would still be full of love for them. He knew the souls of those around him.

He represents what I would like to be – a man who can bring joy and peace to others, a person who can help others have hope when things become difficult, to trust life and God when despair wants to ruin them. He is a model for me.

— Ron Stegman

Why are we drawn to those who have a joyful and forgiving spirit?

Do I wish to be a person that brings hope, peace, and meaning?

Do I ever think of someone as a reflection of God? What does that mean to me?

Divorce

When my parents divorced, I was seven years of age. When I think about this event, I become that age again. One day I am living with my mother, my father, my younger sister, and brother. Then, it seems, the next day, my father and siblings are not there, and I am living in a two-room apartment with my mother. I am alone. Now I realize I was afraid and confused, but then I could not verbalize my feelings nor understand what had happened.

No one said a word to me to explain what was going on. In a sense I was on my own as a seven-year-old. I just thought, "This is the way life is." In writing this some 60 years later, I can still feel the need to cry over the loss and for that little boy. I did not understand, nor, apparently, did anyone else. I have carried this experience throughout my life.

— a friend

What childhood events have impacted my life today?

Can I recall feelings earlier in my life that I still carry within me? Do I need to talk about them?

Words of a Four-Year-Old

Mom: Did Daddy feed you dinner?

Child: Yep!

Mom: Oh, good. What did he give you?

Child: I had one whole lollipop!

Child: Do you know what God is?

Mom: Yes. Do you know what God is?

Child: Yeah! I do!

Mom: What is it? Who is He?

Child: He's the magnet squares that I throw all over. And the toys over there.

Mom: Do you want a pickle and cheese sandwich?

Child: Yeah! But no cheese. Just the pickles on it. And can I have a pickle first before my pickle sandwich?

Child: Mom, will you sing me "Twinkle, Twinkle Little Star"?

Mom: Yes, of course, but you have to close your eyes now.

Child: I don't want to. There are monsters in my eyes.

Mom: When my daughter plays by herself, she reflects on what she and I did that day or week. She will act things out that happened or things we talked about. This morning she's saying, "I'm losing my mind! I can't do this!"

— Evvy Wren Roberts

The innocence of children. What have children taught me?

When do I first remember being a little child? What did I say or do?

Creatures

I am overwhelmed by the beauty and abundance of life as I sit here. I watch ducks and a small bird at the grotto next to the river. Then I watch a tiny ant. I see a turkey display his magnificent tail feathers as he attempts to attract a hen. All of them seem to possess a grace and calmness, which, for some reason, most humans seem to lack.

On the other hand, I feel a sadness as I recall all the creatures I have seen in my life and wish I were still a part of their lives. Somehow, I think, they must still live, and we are somehow one. Somehow in God we become one.

I regret what I did as a young boy. I had a BB gun and would shoot innocent birds for sport. Then I did not give these actions much thought. Some adults should have stopped me. Now I feel great remorse and sadness over my actions toward these small creatures. One time I even shot a young robin who was just beginning to fly. That foolish act haunts me to this day. Another time, when older, I shot a beautiful fox. I can still see this fox look at me as if to say, "Why did you do this?" That, too, haunts me after all these years.

I ask all these creatures for forgiveness and hope to be with them in a new way.

— Ron Stegman

When we harm nature, we harm ourselves. How can I be a person who helps nature?

Do I feel a connection with various creatures? How or when?

What special memory do I have of a pet or animal?

5150 and the Negotiator

There are few things more interesting than watching SWAT do their thing. My younger brother is no longer an active member, but he is now head of the hostage negotiation team. When other SWAT guys accuse him of selling out, he just tells him that his real job is to tell the hostage taker, "Hey, SWAT is outside, and they don't believe you're armed. Would you mind coming to the window and showing them your weapon?"

In truth, my brother is a great negotiator. On my first ever ride along with him in a patrol car, we received an Officer Needs Assistance call. There is nothing quite like a 100 mile-per-hour blast through the city to get your adrenaline pumping. We arrived to find a number of officers facing a 5150 (cop lingo for a disturbed individual). This man was holding a butcher knife to the throat of a terrified woman and screaming death threats interspersed with biblical quotations.

The cops already on scene had their side arms drawn but not pointed at the suspect, due to the hostage's proximity. They were all yelling, "Drop the knife, release the woman! Do it NOW!" Even I could see the suspect was rapidly losing what little control he had. That's when my brother stepped forward.

He unexpectedly began to counter the 5150's quotes with appropriate New Testament verse of his own. This got the man's attention immediately and, right in the middle of a hostage situation, these two proceeded to have a theological discussion. I was riveted for two reasons. First, I was amazed at how quickly the 5150 became considerably more rational, simply because someone was talking with him instead of yelling at him. Second, I wondered just where my very Jewish brother had learned so much about the New Testament.

Well, the two traded quotes for a while before my brother asked, "Do you know the old saying that the meek shall inherit the earth?" The 5150 vigorously nodded his head. "I want you to take the most important step of your life, right here and now. I want you to become one of the meek, so you can inherit the earth. Drop the knife and let this poor woman go – she's done nothing to you, and you've got her scared half to death."

The man's face grew thoughtful. My brother had set the hook – now he sunk it deep. Indicating his fellow officers, he said, "These guys don't understand what I'm talking about, but I know you do." I shot a look at the other cops, who did look pretty discombobulated. I'm sure I did, too.

The 5150 weighed my brother's words before replying, "I'll do it, but only if I can go with you." My brother gave his solemn oath that he would handle all the details: cuffing the man, transporting him to the police station, booking him, and personally placing him in a holding cell. This, of course, is what my brother had wanted all along. The man dropped the knife, surrendering peacefully on the spot.

My brother's quick thinking may have well saved a life that day, perhaps two. But it left me puzzled. I mean, was my brother a genius? Or did he have just a touch of 5150 in himself? Whatever the answer may be, I say again that my brother is a talented negotiator.

— Mark Ozeroff

Do I see love in this story?

Do I try to understand what is going on with others?

Do I talk about my feelings when I struggle?

What special qualities does this negotiator possess?

The Easter Vigil

In the Catholic church, the night before Easter there is a very long period of prayer followed by a mass called the Easter Vigil. In the first part are many scripture readings, which take a considerable amount of time. So, I decided I would arrive late and miss most of the readings. I entered the church through a basement door and was headed upstairs, when a young woman stopped me. I thought, "Oh no, she wants money, and I need to go to the vigil."

She had a frantic look on her face, and she said, "I am trying to rent an apartment for my young son and myself, but the renter will not let me unless I make a deposit. Will you please help us?" I did not have any cash with me, and I said so. Then she asked if we could go up to the church and ask people there for help. I could see the desperation, but I told her, "No, we cannot do that."

I called my wife, and she recommended that I go to a nearby ATM and draw out the money. So, I said, "Wait here, and I'll be right back." I could still see the desperate look on her face. I left to withdrawal the money and when I returned, she was still waiting. I gave her the money and I could see the relief. She then said, "What can I do to pay you in return?"

I answered, "Just pray for me."

When I went into the church, the readings were still going on. The best part of this Easter Vigil was meeting this young woman. I was not only celebrating, but I was also putting Easter into action by passing on care and compassion. It gave me new life as I was able to give love to someone else. It took on the true life-giving experience of Easter.

— Ron Stegman

What would I do if I met this woman?

Do I look for opportunities to serve and love others?

Do Re Mi

When my daughter was a little girl, she always asked me to ask her an "animal question" when I tucked her into bed at night. Usually, the question was along the lines of, "How many animals can you name that start with the letter 'L'?" Eventually I had exhausted all 26 letters of the alphabet and, when I still saw my sweet little girl lying in bed awaiting her question, I had to get creative.

"What is a male deer called?" I asked. She needed a hint, so I said, "It's also a slang word that means dollar bill."

"Buck!" she cried.

"Right!" I said, smiling a proud father's smile. "Now, what do we call a female deer?"

After some time, it was clear that a hint would be necessary. Her musician father thought of a foolproof hint that was certain to elicit a correct response. I cleared my throat and launched into the immortal song from *The Sound of Music*, omitting the first word of the chorus, as it was the answer to the question. "Hmmm, a deer, a female deer..."

As I awaited her response, my daughter's eyes grew wide with excitement. She knew the answer and out it came. "Re!"

If I weren't already in love with my little girl, the mixture of emotions flooding over me at that moment would surely have left me smitten. Trying not to laugh, I said, "That's right honey! Re is right."

I kissed her forehead, turned out the lights, and hurried to a part of the house where my laughter could not be heard. Wiping away the last of my tears, I thought to myself that if our Father in heaven looks at me the way I looked at my innocent little angel when she offered what was a perfectly reasonable answer, I'll do alright when I meet my maker.

Several months later, we went to the zoo and saw a few antelope gathered in a field. My daughter asked, "Which ones are the Res?" At that point, I provided the correct term, but I'm still chuckling to this day.

— Stacey Woolley

What does this story show me about the innocence of children?

What experiences of childhood have remained with me?

Does my love forgive mistakes?

3

RON: Now that we had the land and had purchased the logs, we had to have the logs delivered. That 40-foot flatbed truck had to come up our tiny gravel road with a difficult turn around the creek and they couldn't make the turn. Right away we found out what good neighbors we had. They came with their big tractors and unloaded some of the logs. They pushed the truck with their tractors, helping it make the sharp turn. At the top of the hill we said, "Okay, unload the logs here." They started, and I wanted to look at each one as they took them off to make sure they were sound and not rotted under all that filth.

MICHELE: As the delivery men stacked the logs, Ron insisted they put little strips of wood across as spacers so that air would get to all of them. I was surprised at how particular they were about how they stacked them and how they listened to what we had asked.

RON: The logs then sat there for a year with a big plastic tarp over them. We didn't have enough money to start building yet, and we didn't know how to go about getting started. And the logs still looked crummy because they were covered with all of that junk from the original build. People would visit the property and say, "What are you going to do with these?" We replied, "Build a house!" But we knew nothing about building.

MICHELE: People thought we were crazy. His parents and my parents were just kind of shaking their heads like, "Okay…" We were, too, a little.

RON: After that year of doing nothing with the logs, we had saved a couple thousand dollars, so we started to think, How much will it cost to build this house? We still didn't want any debt! How naïve could we have been?

We contacted a builder in Cincinnati who said, "Pouring the foundation and putting up the logs will cost twenty-six thousand dollars." This was far from the amount of money we had saved. We said, "Oh my, we're going to have to go into debt!"

MICHELE: We contacted another builder and he estimated something like $18,000 or $19,000. We asked people in the area who they would recommend, and everyone told us the same thing. "Oh, you need to talk to Roy. He is a local guy." We contacted him and he gave us a bid of $16,000. That was the cheapest bid so far, but we didn't know how to move forward. We asked him, "Do we sign a contract or what?"

He suggested, "You can sign a contract if you want, but you will probably be better off just paying me for time and materials. I'll start building. I'll give you a bill at the end of each month and you pay me, and we'll just keep doing it that way."

We agreed. After all, we had that $2,000 saved. We just hoped we could save enough as we went along to cover what we would owe him each month. Five dollars an hour for him and four other people, so twenty-five dollars an hour for all of them. It was a risk, but we thought we could do it.

RON: So, we told him to start. We would save up to pay him at the end of each month. He took our word, we took his.

Uno: Cockatiel, Shana Stegman

Uno

I wanted an African Grey parrot. They're some of the world's smartest birds. They can learn to do complicated tasks, show wonderful memory skills, and even communicate with you in human words. They can have the vocabulary of a child, and I thought it would be amazing to have a pet that I could actually talk to in my own words. I find birds fascinating and wanted to learn what a talking parrot could teach me.

I looked up bird rescues in my area. The closest spot was about a two-hour drive from where I lived. I drove up to the rescue, hoping to volunteer for a day, meet some animals, and see what kinds of big, exotic parrots they had. They were wonderful when I got there, giving me a tour and showing me what loving people they were. It was just a couple who had a huge passion for saving animals and had started this most wonderful shelter. I could feel how full of love it was. Even with the huge menagerie of creatures, they were all special. Everything from ponies to pot-bellied pigs and iguanas hung out alongside the other animals of the "bunny barn," which included most of the birds, guinea pigs, cats, and, of course, the bunnies.

Most of the birds there were parakeets and cockatiels – pet store animals that get purchased for $25 while people have no idea how to care for them for the most part. When people realize, hey, birds are really loud and messy and "NO" is certainly never part of their vocabulary, they get sent to a shelter like this one. Another problem is hoarding. People who have good intentions of "saving" these animals will get cages full and then can't take care of them all. They get confiscated and shelters get sent a huge bunch of birds. The shelter has to feed them, care for them, and heal their physical and emotional wounds.

There was one such cockatiel in the bunny barn in a cage alone, while most were caged in groups. He was missing one eye and had a definitive twinkle in the other. His name was Uno and they told me what a joy he was to everyone. He had also come from a hoarding situation with multiple birds, and he hadn't been cared for properly. He had lost his eye most likely in a fight with another bird and had been at the shelter for nearly two years due to the "ugly" eye.

I loved him. I asked if I could hold him, but he was cage bound, which means a bird has been traumatized to the point that they prefer the comfort of their cage to a larger, scarier surrounding area. They got him out for me anyway, which involved lots of squawking and flapping around the bunny barn, stirring up all the other creatures. Finally, he perched cautiously on my arm, not quite trusting me, but perhaps feeling it was the best option at the time. He kept his one eye trained on me, warning me to make a move, and when I would move the tiniest bit, off he would go once again.

I didn't know exactly why, but I needed that bird. He didn't trust me, he had one eye, he was a cockatiel (nothing near an African Grey), and he would need a lot of time and patience to trust anyone at all. But he had that twinkle in his eye and a fight in him that I could relate to. I took him home that day.

A year and a half later, I couldn't imagine my life without that bird. He taught me so much in many ways. He didn't even know what sadness meant, despite all he had been through. "If the sun rises today, we sing!" That was his most important philosophy. Yes, he was always fearful, although we developed a certain trust with one another. But if he ever got mad or scared from his past, he was sure to brush it off with a song within minutes. If I cried, he sang. If I came home yelling and hating life, he sang. If no one paid enough attention to him, he really sang.

Uno loved himself. Completely. He thought he was the most handsome bird anyone had ever seen. The only toys he would accept (no matter how much money I spent on toys) were a cluster of bells and a mirror. The bells were used to accompany his self-written melodies, mostly jam sessions loosely based on the "Andy Griffith" theme song. The bells were also to be worn as hats, carefully placed by putting his head beneath a bell and slowly raising up

Ron Stegman

until it was on his head like a top hat. The mirror is where he did his morning dance each day, impressing himself with his puffed-up chest, raised up wings, and fancy choreography.

Birds regurgitate for one another as signs of affection, and sometimes they will regurgitate on an owner they are particularly bonded with. Uno, however, only regurgitated for himself. He would eat more than his fill, then turn to the mirror and let himself know how much he was loved. Then he eats his own regurgitation, because it would be rude to turn down such admiration.

Uno also wanted to be friends with everyone and every creature. The cat was his best friend, the dog was his best friend, every guest in our home was his best friend. He performed concerts for hours at every party we had, and when we went to the vet, he befriended each and every animal and human inside, like it or not.

The most important lesson I learned from Uno is this: Animals may not speak the same way we do, but the important thing to remember is that they also don't listen the same way. Perhaps we need to learn to listen like an animal before we try to speak to them.

I was frustrated many times when I first brought Uno home. I had never had trouble communicating with an animal before. Mostly I had had cats, and they respond with purrs and chirps and meows to everything I say. They work hard to communicate with their owners. Rubbing your ankles, meowing for treats, leading you to their dish when it's empty. When I got Uno, he sang and sang, but when I answered, he stopped. I can't whistle very well, so I failed to live up to his impressive talents, and when I talked to him, he seemed to find it very boring.

Finally, I realized that as loud and boisterous as Uno was, he spent much more time listening than he did speaking. When he would sing and I would talk and he stopped singing, he was not ignoring me. He was listening, he was learning, he was taking in a new communication. He actually wanted to know what I was saying and why. He would tilt his head to the side and take it in. He sang a lot, and he had his demanding chirps, angry chirps, and happy chirps. But all of those chirps basically meant, "I want to interact with you. I want you to listen to me and then I want to listen to you."

I had planned on having an amazing African Grey who could have full conversations with me about the weather and what puzzle he had learned to complete that day. But I realized that even the birds that speak our words are doing it because it meets the same goal as Uno's. It's fun to get the reaction, the treat, the praise. They are smart enough to know that this keeps us interacting with them.

It's the same thing Uno did when he pretended to be distressed to get me in the room. He would scream as if he was in extreme pain until I ran in to check on him, and then he would sing happily. Or he would stick his little talon up his nose to induce a sneezing fit, so I would think he was on his death bed. Then he could share his newest musical composition with me. He used a human emotion to get me in there with him, then he could continue to communicate with me in his special way. No matter what form they use, they still speak and listen as a bird does, and that can go unnoticed if you only use human words. I'm so lucky I got a tone-deaf, one-eyed cockatiel instead of my majestic parrot. He taught me to listen.

— Kira King

Uno taught lessons to his keeper. What has a pet or animal taught me?

Why are many people so drawn to different animals?

How has a pet or animal helped me to grow emotionally?

If I could be an animal, what would I be and why?

The Gift of a Brother

The most loving moment in my life has to be the day my brother was born. For twelve years I was the only child until this day. It was a cold winter day. I was at school, and my mother was due to have the baby that day. I carried around my father's beeper all day so that he could call me when the baby was born. It was near the end of the day, and the whole school was in anticipation. I was getting ready to board the bus when the beeper went off.

When my dad said it was a boy, everyone in the entire school went crazy. I thought I felt proud then but it didn't compare to later that night. I went to the hospital after I ate dinner. When I walked in and saw my mother holding my brother I almost started crying. At no point in my life have I felt more love for my family than I did right there. It was a very moving experience.

— written by a high school student for **Family Memories**

Imagine! This twelve-year-old boy understands the gift of life, the gift of a family. Have I felt this way in my life?

How am I grateful? What gifts and what people do I have in my life?

The Singer

We were walking on a dirt street in Matamoros, Mexico on a scorching, humid, summer day when we heard a man singing. His was a fantastic voice. His voice filled the dirty streets and made the surroundings almost comfortable. My wife approached the singer and asked him if he was a professional singer. He smiled and answered no. He could have been. Before us was this very talented man in this poor, hot *colonia* with a wonderful voice and joyful spirit. There are so many amazing human beings who are unseen. There are so many who live in extremely difficult situations and yet are very gifted and unknown.

At times, when I am around poverty or difficult living conditions, I wonder if there is a God. However, when I experience the dignity of the poor, like this singer, and when I witness the gifts of the forgotten people, then I experience meaning.

— Ron Stegman

What talents do I have which can brighten the world?

Do I appreciate the gifts of others even when they do not? And do I tell them?

A Remarkable Woman

I stand in awe of my friend. In spite of a harsh, abusive, poverty ridden upbringing, she has dedicated herself to helping current victims of abuse and neglect. She is a volunteer at a rape crisis and domestic violence center. Several nights a month, she is on call and if that pager goes off, she is up and to the hospital to meet with a rape or violence victim, helping them through their ordeal and keeping them informed of what will happen next. If the case goes to trial, she sits right beside that victim during the whole procedure, explaining the "legalese" and giving support to the person.

Sometimes helping victims of abuse means making cookies, which she took to police stations across the county when she went to explain to the officers just what a victim of rape or violence needs when the police are called. The cookies, she said with a smile, were to get the officers' attention, making them more receptive to her message.

Friends wouldn't recognize her without her "tag-along" friend – her oxygen tank. She has never smoked but she has four lung diseases, including COPD and emphysema. She also has an internal morphine pump to help her cope with the constant pain from a work injury which crushed her shoulder. Her health was so bad ten years ago that the doctors gave her six months to live. But she is a fighter, for herself and others.

In spite of her physical problems, she is always "up" and cheerful, always ready to lend a friend a hand, ready with a sympathetic shoulder. When I am upset about a problem, she is someone I can turn to, someone who will listen. Even though her problems far outweigh mine, she makes me feel that my problems are worth her time and compassionate ear.

She is a blessing to her family, cooking wonderful meals and making sure her husband always has a drink, food, and a cell phone when he goes out to cut wood. She also takes delight in her three grandchildren, babysitting when called on. There isn't a stray cat or dog that comes her way without getting its share of love, care, food, and a visit to the vet.

She credits her faith in God and her marriage in helping her overcome her own abuse. She believes in forgiveness, love, and helping others instead of becoming bitter and blaming.

— Michele Stegman

A humble woman of service in spite of life's challenges. Who do I know who gives service and love so freely?

From where does such a person as this receive the strength to do these things?

What handicap do I have that keeps me from living fully? How do I overcome this?

Affection

The greatest area in which I need to grow in relationship with women is romance. I guess you could also call it my gentle side. I feel that, because my family does not show emotions and affection very openly, I have been hindered in showing affection towards women. Often, I feel awkward when girls approach me in an affectionate way. I feel as though I may hurt them with my strength if I try to embrace them. Many times, I feel as if I intimidate them with my size and I scare them off. I am beginning to improve on this in my relationship. My girlfriend has helped. I need to get past this fear in order to be able to show affection more with her and later in life so my wife knows that I love her, and our children will not be afraid to show their emotions.

— written by a high school student for **Family Memories**

What hinders me from showing affection and sharing emotions?

Do I fear rejection if I show my feelings or deeper side?

Why do we remember emotion-filled events so easily?

What special times do I remember?

A Dog and Baby

Ender was a wonderful dog. He loved to go snowboarding with his owners, chase a frisbee, and go everywhere they went. Most of all, he loved to jump into the cold river to chase a stick and bring it to shore. He always set the stick down and shook himself dry before taking the stick back for another toss. He learned early not to shake himself off close to people.

When his owners had a baby, things changed. As the baby began to find her legs, Ender began losing his. As she began to stand on wobbly legs and take hesitant steps, Ender also stood on wobbly legs and found it harder and harder to get up. As the baby learned to walk, Ender could no longer walk at all. Unlike the baby, who now trotted about quite well, Ender's back legs would not work.

One day, his owner took him to the river, tossed a stick not far from shore, then supported him in the water so he could fetch the stick. It was a faint shadow of what he had once been able to do, but it brought him joy.

Every day the baby watched her parents lift Ender up, wrapped in a blanket, so they could carry him to and from the car together. One day, they noticed the baby at play with her plastic animals. She took her toy wolf, placed it tenderly on a piece of fabric, and carried it around, much as they had done for Ender.

Now, at 16 months at age, this baby is Ender's legs. She hugs him and shares her snacks with him. One day her mother gave her a drink of water and when she turned back around, the baby was giving it to Ender. She pushes his water bowl close and fills it with cups of water. Sometimes, she even holds a cup of water for him to drink. She knows he needs special care and tries to help. As her mother said, "It kind of broke our hearts, but it made our hearts grow bigger, too."

— Michele Stegman

Life is joyous, life is sad. How do I feel about living with both?

Children learn behavior by watching us. What did I learn from my home as a child? How have I influenced the behavior of children around me?

Was my self-esteem helped or hindered by others?

Raccoon Story

Driving down my street on a cold winter day, I noticed something sitting in the road. Curled up, puffy, shivering, I thought it may be a cat. I stopped and honked my horn as I always do, hoping to scare the little thing off. It picked up its head and looked at me. A raccoon. Instead of running, he simply lowered his head back down onto the pavement. Please, no, was my first thought. I had long ago sworn to never leave an animal in the road no matter what. I stop for every turtle, snake, dog, blowing leaf that resembles a scurrying animal (fall is a very stressful season for me) and make sure to do everything I can to assure their safety.

I told myself getting out of the car was a bad idea. It's a wild raccoon, I reminded myself. Followed by, My parents are going to be so mad if they find out I got bit by a wild raccoon... as I stepped out of the car.

I walked slowly toward him, waving my hands and kicking my boots toward him a bit, telling him in a very logical manner that he needed to get off the road. I explained the dangers of where he was sitting and begged him to get safe because he was important. He didn't budge. I got a bit closer, getting nervous but determined to at least get him to the side of the road. I was shaky. I know animals well and I know what a big hissing raccoon mouth looks like. I also know how fast they can be when they want. This is when he looked up at me. His right eye was sealed shut. It looked to be an eye infection. But his left eye looked into mine and I stopped shaking immediately. There was so much that passed through us in the moment our eyes met. He looked sad, and spent, and as though he had made the decision to give up. He was telling me to give up on him too. He was done.

"Please, little raccoon," I said, "you can be okay, I promise. Just follow me and come to the side of the road. You will get hit if you stay here. You can't just give up."

I went to my trunk and pulled out some old towels I kept there. I piled them on the side of the road on top of all the ice and snow.

Then I went back over to him, and he looked up at me again.

This time his gaze seemed to say, "Can I trust you?"

"Come here," I called, slowly backing up toward the towels. He kept his gaze on mine and took one step closer to me. I jumped and he stopped. We were both testing the waters here. Two "dangerous creatures" in one another's world, trying to guess where we stood, how far we could trust.

I continued to back up and he slowly followed. I spoke soothingly to him the whole time, explaining why he could trust me, keeping my eyes on his. He did the same, and, over the next 15 minutes, we made it to the side of the road. We had gotten a lot of snow, and he was slipping and couldn't climb up on top of it to make it to the towels, so I reached down and made a bridge of towels going up the hill. Once he managed to climb that, he curled up onto the towels. I got another one and carefully placed it on top of him. He put his nose down into the towel, closed his eyes for a moment, and then looked back up at me, thankful.

"This is all I can do for you," I told him. "I'm so sorry, but you're a wild raccoon and I'm a human, and this is all I have. I wish I could do more."

I drove away and ran my errands, all the while desperately calling rescues who, of course, were not willing to take in an injured raccoon. They will take orphaned babies, but adult raccoons are too risky, too vicious, and not endangered. It is too much money and manpower for a nonprofit rescue to go out of their way to help them. I understood but promised to be his lookout to the full extent that I could.

When I came back later that day, he was curled up on the edge of the towels, covered in snow. It was snowing pretty hard then, and we were expected to get up to five inches. A few kids were getting off the bus from school and they asked me if he was dead. I told them he was just hurt but that I was going to do my best to take care of him. The one boy said, "I hope you can save him. I love animals and if it wasn't a raccoon I would bundle him up and take him home."

The child's father then pulled up and asked me if I needed help. He offered to bring me food and water because he could see I was not going to leave this animal. Just the offer meant so much when most people drove by, almost hitting me and my new friend.

By now, the towels were soaked through. When I got near him, he got up to try to walk to me and fell back into the road. He put his head down once again: "I give up." My heart dropped. I ran back to my house and got a big box, more dry towels, cat food, and water. I brought it all back and set it up for him. But he couldn't pick himself up from the road. His injuries weren't extensive, but he was cold, he was tired, and he was losing hope.

I took a stick and tried to push him up the little hill. It didn't work. Bracing myself for the hospital phone call for rabies shots, I wrapped one of the towels around my hand and slowly reached to his back, touching him gently near the bottom. He relaxed and allowed me to reach under his body, lifting him up to the ledge. He didn't turn his head to bite, he didn't hiss, but when I set him down by the box, he instead tried to climb into my lap. He followed my hand as I put out the food and water, attempting to nuzzle it. I thought maybe I was crazy. A wild raccoon trying to get me to pet him? Wanting to be on my lap? I stayed as careful as I could and kept pulling my hand away, explaining to him why that couldn't be. But as he ate his food, I wrapped a towel around my hand and pet his back. And he lay down, paws in the food dish, eyes on mine, warm in his box.

It was hard to leave him there and of course I checked on him again later. He was curled up in the box sleeping, safely out of the snow. All night I worried and cried about his safety. My boyfriend questioned my sanity more than once (although he took a picture of the raccoon safely curled up on his way home from work to show me). The next morning, I brought him more food and water, and saw that someone had added to his shelter.

They had put a big trash can with a pillow inside next to the box and draped a blanket connecting

Ron Stegman

the two areas to make him a sort of fort. I wanted to cry for the good of humanity. To see that someone else had cared enough for a raccoon to do this made me so happy. It also took away some of the burden that I was the sole person trying to save this animal's life.

The raccoon was nowhere to be seen, but it was obvious he had rested out the snowy night in safety and he had eaten some of the food. I still keep an eye out in that area every day, but I haven't seen him since. I like to think he got enough rest and shelter to recover and find a safer spot for himself. But no matter what happened, I know that for a few moments we both saw the connection between the spirits of all nature and creation, and when we are at our lowest points, sometimes we are helped by the least likely of that creation. Those we are taught to fear sometimes become our salvation, those we learn to hate can prove to love.

This isn't simply a story about saving a raccoon, it's a story about having faith in one another, and doing whatever we can to better the life of any living thing. We truly are all one in this world.

— Kira King

What do I think about this person going to so much trouble for a small animal?

How does it affect me if a creature is hurting?

New Mother

Every day I feel stronger toward her. In the beginning I didn't know what to think. It was so surreal. I knew that I loved her and cared for her. Now I can't stand to be away from her. I see how perfect she is and I'm so proud of her. I didn't know I could be so proud of a newborn baby. I'm waiting for something about her to just be ordinary.

When she cries, I feel like I'm failing as a parent. If she cries for half a second, I feel awful that she has to go through any pain. She's too innocent to go through any hurt. But when I'm able to bring her in close, soothe her, and feed her the world comes together again. I remember I'm capable of making her happy and caring for her.

I want my life to be calm for her sake. I want her to be around peace. I hope she always feels that she can make her own decisions, even as a child, and become a better adult because of it.

I can't stop looking at her, but it's almost too overwhelming to watch her because I love her so much. If I haven't held her for a few minutes, I have to see her again to believe that this is real. That she is my daughter and I get to keep her.

— Shana Stegman

What do I think are good qualities of a parent?

Did I feel loved and supported as a child?

Have I ever felt overwhelmed with love?

The Gift of Simplicity

I was a caretaker at a ranch with a bed and breakfast. A guest asked me the other day if my parents thought I was crazy because of the type of life I have chosen. She said, "As beautiful as the ranch is, and how much fun it seems to be to live here and care for the animals, your parents must think you are crazy. How can anyone survive without a corporate job?" This made me laugh and feel sorry for her at the same time.

While she was feeling pity for me because I did not have millions of dollars, I told her that I became this way because of my parents. If I'm crazy, then I must have gotten that from them. They both have taught me the love for nature and animals. I told her this is how I feel most comfortable and that I probably would not fit in in the corporate world. I thank my parents for helping me see the world outside of business and money.

Although it might be fun to have a lot of money, I think she is the one missing out. My parents are two of the best and kindest people I know, and I am proud to be just like them. I should have said to her that if it were not for my way of life, and people like me, she would not be able to be served on her vacations.

— Shana Stegman

What brings me true happiness beyond work and money?

When I die, how would I like to be remembered?

Do I enjoy the work I am doing? What would make me feel the most fulfilled?

Dictator

Reading about dictators in world history I concluded that there are certain behavior patterns and similar thinking. Or so it seems to me. From Genghis Khan, Attila the Hun, Napoleon, Pol Pot, Peron, Idi Amin, Adolph Hitler, and others, here are some of the patterns and various ways of doing things.

They are narcissists, sociopaths, power seekers. Often charismatic speakers, they want control. They want order and obedience in the people they rule. They demand this order and uniformity in the people. Law and order are essential, as long as it is their type of law and order. They control the central government, the people, the laws. All must march to their wishes, their commands. And they will say this is for the good of all, for the nation's welfare. They will use lies and deception.

The military must be totally committed to them. The state, in a sense, is them. There is always a threat of reprisal for any challenges or questioning of their rule.

The dictator often causes thousands and thousands to be persecuted, jailed, killed. How then does he retain power?

Why are such men able to rule, and even have millions follow them? Why allow such oppression, such evil to rule them? Fear? Security? Ignorance? Nationalism? Do most people just follow the group, the crowd leader?

— a friend

Have I ever been made to follow the rules without question? When and why? Did I have feelings about this?

Do I feel that I have the freedom to be the type of person that I want to be?

Ron Stegman

A Mayan Priest

A missioner was talking to a Mayan priest in Guatemala who said he and his wife have separate beds at holy times. The wife said their knees better not touch. If anything happens between them, there will be storms, wind, and lightning, and the corn will be blown over.

That very night there was a terrible storm, and the corn was blown over. The next day, the missioner asked the priest what happened. The priest said, "It was not us. That priest over on the next hill does not keep the rule." He pointed out that marriage is not just for the two in it, but that it affects all those around them.

— a missionary friend

How have my relationships affected others?

What are the qualities that attract me to others?

To Dad

I love you for eating all my candy bars, Dad.

I got out "Hoppy" today. He's the little ceramic bunny I won as a prize for selling a whole box – 20 – of candy bars. I was only about five years old, but I remember getting my box of candy from a man who came door to door. I think I sold three or four of those candy bars to aunts or uncles, but I know who bought the rest. I remember you taking the candy bars and me insisting on the nickel. I remember looking in that box and seeing the nickels pile up and the candy disappear. I was so happy when the man came back, and I got to choose my prize. I still treasure that little bunny and I treasure the memory of how I got it. Thanks, Dad, for eating all my candy bars.

— Michele Stegman

A simple act can have a lasting effect on someone. Do I have an experience like this that has stayed with me?

Has someone thanked me for something I said or did in the past that I didn't realize meant so much to them?

Feelings stay with us. Do I have a feeling that was a result of a small act or event?

Ron Stegman

Quarts of Beer

My father was a quiet, rather gentle man who worked hard. That is, until he had a few quarts of beer. Then he became an argumentative and nasty man. The change was almost impossible to believe. Those few quarts of beer helped to bring him a mostly sad life.

My mother divorced him when I was seven and my two siblings were younger. Then we were separated. We recall him hitting our mother and, when my young brother lived alone with him, he was neglected because of the drinking. At times, our father would come home inebriated and harass my brother.

He would go to work as a pleasant man, work well with his coworkers, and then, following work, he would drink his quarts and change his personality and demeanor. He was now ready to fight.

Eventually he drove my brother away and then my sister – all because of his drinking.

He died in his late 40s because of smoking, environmental factors, and most likely, because of the quarts of beer in his lonely life. Shortly before he died, my father stated he still loved my mother after all those years. I still feel sad for him as he could have had a loving life and family all around him. He was a good man, but this one weakness took a great part of his life.

— a friend

Do I know others who have a sad or difficult life because of an addiction?

Am I able to forgive those who have hurt me or others because of their own struggles?

Do I have habits that cause me to change or become less full of life?

4

MICHELE: We had already paid somebody else to dig the foundation and he tried to cheat us. Right in the middle of digging, he upped the price for no reason!

RON: We told him, "Stop working. We don't have the money." Right then and there, he changed his mind, and appeared to feel guilty. He said, "I wouldn't just leave you high and dry," and went back to the original price and finished the job. Later on, he even helped us with the interior of the house. He told us he had an old barn and said we could have the siding. We ended up using that for some of the walls on the inside of the house.

MICHELE: As they were digging, they made it eight feet down and hit a sheet of solid rock. That is what our house is sitting on. There is a Biblical story about a person who built a house on sand versus a person who built on solid rock. We were on solid rock! This was very significant to me that we were building our house not only on this actual rock but also on the foundation of our relationship with God.

RON: They poured the foundation and we went out when it was drying. We wrote our names, the date, and a dedication of the house to God in the cement.

MICHELE: Our contractor, Roy, had asked, "How big is this house going to be?" We answered, "It's 20 by 40 feet," so they poured the foundation to that exact size. We decided we wanted a fireplace on the east end of the house. To make space to put in the fireplace, he had to split the logs. As he was putting up the logs, Roy told me, "It's a good thing you decided to put the fireplace at the east end because it turns out this original house was not exactly 20 by 40. If we hadn't split the logs on this end, it wouldn't have fit on the foundation."

I guess the pioneers who originally built the place didn't worry too much about precise measurement! Nothing in our house is square or straight. From the outside, you can see that the walls are a bit crooked. But to me, it just makes this place that much more special and unique.

RON: As we were building, we found that one 40-foot log and two of the base logs were rotten. The man we bought them from was true to his word and volunteered to pay to have them replaced. Then someone told me a barn had been knocked down by a storm and they had extra logs to sell. I went to where the barn had been and bought three of those logs for twenty dollars. Roy was able to fit them together to replace the missing logs.

We had no idea how they were going to lift these logs and place them, but Roy was so creative that it became simple. They rigged a boom on a backhoe and connected a chain. They wrapped the chain around the logs and hoisted them up to set them in place. Old log cabins were not usually very big, so we were surprised at how large it was as it began coming together.

Once the logs were all up, Roy asked, "How do you want to lay out this house?" We stood out in the grass, trying to imagine our future home. He pointed out a section to us. "Here's a space for a big window."

"That's good. Cut it."

"Okay, what other windows?"

While we stood there in the grass of what would be our front yard, we decided where the doors and windows would be.

MICHELE: In the original disassembled house, there were three doors and a window in the front. We didn't need three doors and I wondered why the pioneers had so many. We combined one door and a window into a picture window. As I stood looking out that big hole, I thought of how wonderful it would be to someday stand there and watch the snow come down. I didn't realize just how much snow I would watch come down, because our first winter there was 1976-1977 when all the blizzards hit!

We kept the door in the middle. The third door was made it into another window. So, we did change the original plan of the house and rearranged those logs to make it work. We would go out every day and the logs would be higher, and we were excited as they went up and up. Then one day I went out and they were lower. In dismay I asked, "What happened?"

Roy said, "I didn't like the way they were going together. We're going to do this again and do it right."

RON: Roy was so affordable and precise with his work that we asked him to also put the roof on. I had planned to do it myself, but I knew nothing!

We wanted this home to be authentic, and that included the roof, which didn't come with the numbered logs or the plan. We didn't want something modern, like asphalt shingles, on an old house. The pioneers used wooden shakes, so I searched for cedar shakes for the roof and Roy put them on.

Again, he allowed us to pay by the month. We saved and when he gave us the bill, we always had enough. We knew somewhat how many hours they were putting in, but it was still amazing that every month we managed to set aside exactly what we needed.

MICHELE: He was such a craftsman, and he did so many little things that we didn't even ask him to do. By the time he was done, we had paid him not $16,000, as he first asked, but $11,800.

Maurice: Jumping Spider, Roy King

Jumping Spiders

One morning, when I was watering the little potted plant on the kitchen windowsill, a hairy face with lots of eyes popped over the rim of the pot, seemingly choking and coughing. It was a jumping spider. She had been hiding in the pot until I unwittingly almost drowned her.

Now, I know some people are terror stricken when they see a spider. I happen to like them. They do so much good. And since jumping spiders do not make large webs and are not harmful to humans, they are welcome in my house.

This one was shy but had taken up residence in the kitchen. When I would come over to the counter, she would run and hide, peeping out at me from behind a canister or whatever was sitting there. I told her I would not intentionally hurt her, but she remained careful. Curious, but cautionary.

I began to find dead insects on the windowsill. Mainly flies. This was summer and we live in the country, with doors opening a lot. I was glad my little friend was there.

As time went on, however, I noticed that she wasn't quite as quick. Even when we shooed flies over to her, she rarely caught one. She was getting thinner and one day I found her dead.

A few days later I came into the kitchen and there was another jumping spider. I was glad to see him. But he was so different from the first one. This new spider was not shy. I would begin making bread and he would boldly march out onto the counter to see what I was doing, often getting flour all over his little face. I would try to shoo him away from danger, but he just thought I wanted to play, watching my fingers in fascinating, coming closer to see, and not afraid at all. I imagined that these two were mother and son, but I had no way to know for sure. It was just the way it seemed to me.

These spiders taught me a wonderful lesson. I was amazed at their different personalities. But here were two tiny creatures that most people would have smashed without thought who both showed curiosity, friendliness, and distinct personalities.

— Michele Stegman

What are my reflections after reading these stories?

Life is full of wonder even in tiny jumping spiders. What fills me with wonder and amazement as I observe small creatures living their quiet life?

Do I recall being fascinated by small bugs, bees, butterflies, or other small creatures when I was young? Do I still feel this way?

Trick or Treat

I took our girls trick-or-treating. As we walked along in a rather nice neighborhood, I noticed a house that was a bit run down. It needed paint, there were weeds growing in the yard, and toys and tools were scattered about. For some reason I felt very drawn to that house. I just had a good feeling when I looked at it. As the girls came up to that house, the people came out with costumes on, laughing and smiling, and dug into their stash to put handfuls of candy into the girls' bags. They were so joyful, and I guess it just radiated in some invisible way from the house.

— Michele Stegman

How often do we miss out on a good person or experience because we pre-judge the exterior? Can I think of an example in my own life?

Do I have good feelings about certain places that I can't explain? Have I explored these feelings?

Violence in a Child's Life

The little boy knew he was NOT supposed to be outside. His father and grandfather forbade him to go out the door of his home. His sister and his older brother said never ever be outside when they were home alone. And most days, the children were home alone. Abuelo and Papa were always looking for work so the little boy, his sister, and two brothers had to be good when they were by themselves.

On Sundays the family would walk to church. Sundays were the best days because they were all together. The family would walk to church in the morning and afterwards there were tortillas and beans to eat and sometimes rice.

Anyway, just once the boy wanted to be outside. This day was quieter, and things did not seem so bad. The sun was even shining. At night there were bad noises – screaming, yelling and crying. There were loud bangs too. The little boy knew the loud bangs were sometimes firecrackers and sometimes from guns. There were always terrible sounds after the loud bangs. The little boy often slept with his father and brothers in the same bed. His father was a strong man, and it was comforting to be next to him. The bad noises during the night were not so bad when the little boy was next to his father and brothers. The powerful arms and the father's smell were so reassuring to the boy.

The boy remembers his mom holding him, but the memory is not so vivid anymore. His mother left two years ago. She got tired of the poverty and started going out at night. She met another man and decided to leave her husband and children. There was no one to take care of him or his baby brother after the mother left so his older brother and sister did the household chores and babysitting.

The little boy loved school. There were friends and books and paper and pencils. The teacher was pretty and nice. Sometimes one of his friends had a soccer ball to kick around at recess. Today the urge to be outside was so strong. His sister was watching their little brother. The boy felt he could sneak outside for just a little while, and nothing would happen, and he would be just fine.

The little boy opened the door. His big brother saw him but did not say anything. The boy quietly closed the door and sat down on the step. The next-door neighbor was outside working on his motorcycle. The little boy felt safe. The sun was warm. It felt so good to just sit.

The boy saw a black car driving slowly around the corner. He stood up but could not make his feet move. He looked at the neighbor. The man was watching the black car too. The boy had a strange feeling. There was something about this black car that made him feel afraid. The boy's stomach felt bad. His hands tingled and his legs felt heavy. The black car was driving slowly towards him. Something was wrong. The windows were dark. A back window of the car came down. The boy could not see who was in the car. There were loud noises, firecracker noises. The neighbor man fell down and then the black car started driving towards him. The car's back window was still open...the man looked at the boy and pretended to shoot him.

— a friend

This is a true story. How can a child who experiences violence, neglect, or abuse be healed?

What were some of my traumas as a child? What are my feelings in reflecting on this story and why is that my response?

The Funeral

Yesterday I conducted a funeral for a man who was a husband, father, and grandfather. He had died suddenly. They had little church background and yet I saw all of them as very Christian in their service to others and in their love and support for each other. Some worked in public service jobs that risked their lives, one cared for a son with Down's Syndrome, another worked in Africa with AIDS patients. At the man's death, the family donated multiple body parts for the good of others. The father's influence was evident in their lives.

I spoke of hope and his love for them still. I assured them he was with the Creator and close to them. I wanted to give them hope and consolation in the midst of their great pain. Near the end of the prayer service, I watched the family members come up to the bier. This was difficult to see. His wife, during the service, kept her head down in sorrow and grief. She had said, "He was my best friend." They had been married for 52 years. Now she stood there and did not seem to want to leave. The youngest daughter approached and wept with her husband alongside her. The grandson with Down's Syndrome stood there and appeared to be trying to understand what was happening. He was also a source of great comfort to the family and had been very close to his grandfather. Another grandson in his late teens or early 20s wept openly. A third grandson lifted his head upward in anguish.

I wanted the grandfather to be alive again. I personally would have liked to have known this man who left an incredible legacy. I hoped some of my words were with them in their pain. I hoped God would give them some consolation. And I saw their love for one another as a strong support in their grief. He was a remarkable man.

— Ron Stegman

Do I reflect on my own mortality when I hear of a death?

The man left a large legacy of care and service through his children and grandchildren. What do I want to leave my family and the world?

How have I handled the anguish of loss in my life?

Words from a Mother

One time I imagined my mother speaking to me after her death. The following is what I seemed to hear:

My son, I am enthralled with God and love. Never worry about me and others. We are in great union with our beautiful God. It is, of course, beyond human words. My spirit rejoices in all my family, and I continually pray for all of you. I will help you with this decision for next year. God is very close to you in this.

Pray often as the Father has said. Then you will learn the language of love. I am very close to you now and I realize the gifts that I gave to you. Your father also prays for you, and he rejoices in his two grandchildren. How beautiful and loved they are.

We both will always be close to your two children. God loves you. I know you hurt when you think of me and your dad, but we are very close to you. God is with you and knows that you love. Be at peace in the love that dwells in you.

— Ron Stegman

This is unusual indeed. Have I had a similar type of experience? What happened?

What are my thoughts about life after death? Am I a person of hope?

Love Shared

I decided years ago not to have any children of my own. I love kids, but I just didn't feel that it was the right path for me. Over the years, I have feared at times that I made a mistake. Parents will tell you that you do not truly know love until you have a child. I don't believe that to be true, as I am someone who loves very deeply, but there have been times that I wondered if I was missing a part of life by not having a child.

When my sister called to tell me she was pregnant, I was elated and sad at the same time. My sister was my closest friend in the world, and I loved her more than I loved anyone. Now she would get to love her own child and I would become second to her. But I was also so excited to become an aunt. I knew I would give this child all the love I would have given my own.

When my niece was born, I was there to watch her come into the world. In that moment, the second I saw her, I was so overwhelmed with love for her that I thought I would pass out in the delivery room. I had never loved someone so much. I was overcome with the fact that I could love a person this much who I didn't even know yet. I had no idea what her personality would be, what she would look like as she grew, or even if she would love me back. But I knew I loved her absolutely unconditionally. As she has grown up over the past six years, she has made my life so full. Even though she is not my own child, I can feel that we are connected in a special way. I also see my sister in her, and it makes me so happy that some of her traits, expressions, and joy are passed on to this new generation. The fears I had of losing the closeness with my sister were unfounded. Instead, our love has grown deeper and expanded to include three of us. Love is not something that gets taken away or replaced. It just continues to build and expand with every person you let into it.

— a friend

Who or what has enabled me to love more?

Do I put conditions on my love or let it move freely?

Little by Little

Ranchito is a small *colonia*, or neighborhood, just minutes from the U.S. border. One of the main ways the people there make a living is to collect garbage. They have small carts, bicycle or horse drawn, which they use to go around nearby neighborhoods and, for a few cents, take away the garbage from individual homes. They are supposed to take the garbage to the dump, but the dump is so far away, they could not make enough money to live on each day if they took it there. So, they bring the garbage home and dump it in their own streets. Dirt streets. Streets that are impassable because of the garbage which is piled high. Higher than the houses made of old wood, cardboard, tin, and whatever else the people can find.

Some of the people raise pigs, slaughter them, and sell the meat. There are pig bones scattered around the streets, too, and the yards where the pigs live are filled several feet high with manure and dead animals. Skinny, mange-infected dogs wander around.

Another source of income for one woman was *nopalitos*, or cactus leaves, which are a popular food in Mexico. Her tiny back yard was full of prickly pear cactus, and she was sitting there scraping the thorns off some of the wide pad leaves, getting them ready to sell.

We got a glimpse into one home. The "kitchen" was basically an open fire with a piece of metal propped over it for a cook surface. There was a tin roof projecting out from the house, but it was open on three sides. The dirt floor was littered with the remains of past fires and one wall and roof supports were black with old smoke. Two or three pots were the only cooking utensils I saw. I didn't see any food, or a place food could be stored. Inside the home was one small windowless bedroom with two beds and a dirt floor.

The only water source for the neighborhood was a dribbling faucet at the end of each street corner. And the only clean space was an outdoor church. I could not fathom living there. Yet, without fail, each of the people we met were smiling, welcoming, and seemed happy. And when they came to church, they were clean, and their clothes were clean and crisply ironed.

Ron Stegman

I have been to many Third World countries including India, Haiti, Central America, and the Middle East. This was the first time I came away crying my eyes out.

— Michele Stegman

Many in our world live on very little. Do I reach out in some way to others who struggle?

How can people who struggle and have so little still smile and welcome others into their lives with such grace?

Have I experienced poverty in my own life or in the lives of others? Not just physical poverty, but in any way?

View from Above

Looking down from the plane window, there is this play world below. Or so it seems. I see roads with no cars, streets with no people, towns and rivers with no movement, square fields of various colors and shades. There are large bare spots and then green covered areas. I see bodies of water large and small. The fields might be planted with crops.

I am looking out for miles and yet see no movement. Above all this is a light blue sky. What amazes me as I look at these shades of life, geometric figures, straight and crooked roads, bodies of water, is I can see no life, no movement of any kind. Just a planet with no life. Yet I know there are thousands of people in these scenes – moving, breathing, living their daily lives, working, suffering, enjoying, and crying.

I feel for this planet – apprehensive – and I feel for all the people in these scenes. I want them to be blessed in their lives and days. I want them to be happy.

For a time, I am removed from this world as I fly overhead at 35,000 feet. It is as if I am removed from life as I sit here and gaze below. I think when I drop down to the earth, trees, streets, and people, I will have a little more affection and appreciation for the people and their daily lives as well as the gift of the planet Earth.

And too, all this I see is but a small dot in this enormous universe and seems very unimportant in the vast expanse. Yet I know each person below is engaged in life, desiring, loving, hoping, and relating as well as all creatures seeking life. This small planet is important and in this vast universe, there is a light.

— Ron Stegman

Sometimes we need to look at our world from a different perspective. A different culture, different race, different age. Have I done this? What happened?

Do I have feelings for those who are the forgotten?

A New Job

Starting a new job is tough, and I had a lot of doubts about myself in my new role. I was working outdoors with children, using adventures and nature to build their confidence. My very first day, I was talking to a 4th grade boy about accomplishments. He said he was most proud of the fact that he won a soccer tournament two years ago. I said I was proud of my new job. He said, "Well, you're obviously made for this job." I said, "I hope so." He looked right into my eyes, shrugged his shoulders and said simply, "You are."

I thought it was sweet but brushed it off. Yet those words stuck with me the whole week.

Whenever I struggled or felt unsure of myself, I heard the boy's voice telling me I was made for this. I started a job where I set out to help others, and they, in turn, helped me. Sometimes it takes an unexpected voice to remind us of who we are and what we are capable of. I had so many great experiences that week and gained a lot of confidence. And it all started with that small conversation. I must remember to learn from each person and challenge I encounter in my daily life. You never know how much they will mean later.

— Kira King

A word, a touch, a smile can mean so very much to people. Do I give such a gift to others? Who has given me this gift?

Confidence is often gained through encouragement of others. Where do I need encouragement or need to encourage other people?

Community Service Man

In our school the students are given many hours of community service. They have worked with the Special Olympics and mentored students in the inner city at 10 schools. They also worked in a Central American country visiting with orphans who had no one to help them.

Much of this service was inspired by a man who volunteered at the school. This man committed his life to this school for about 25 years. To help the school financially, he worked the Bingo events for 50 weeks a year for all of those years. He was also at every basketball and football game working the concessions stand for those years. If something needed to be done for any school banquet, he was there.

In his 60s, he was diagnosed with cancer and was not expected to live. The students realized what an example and servant he had been. Shortly before his death, he was driven around the field during a football game to honor him and they stopped at the concession stand where he had worked for so many years to give him recognition.

This special man had wanted to be a student at the school years before but could not afford the tuition. Before he died, the school set up a scholarship in his name. His grandson was the first to receive the scholarship.

— a friend

Great love and a quiet manner. Who do I know that has these qualities?

How has the example of another influenced my life?

Do I find myself admiring this man?

Depression and Redemption

I often wondered what it must have been like for Mary to stand at the cross and watch her son suffering and dying. What must she have felt? Two years ago, I found out. I was in such depression that I knew I would die. I was at the home of my parents and sitting in the enclosed porch. I knew my parents loved me but through the years they had seldom said so in words. My mother spoke of her love a little in the many years.

On that day, as I sat on the porch in total defeat, my mother walked out and looked at me. She did not say a word, but she did not need to speak. As I was describing to her how I was feeling I could see in her face her total pain and anguish and love for me. She said everything that I needed her to say without opening her mouth. There was a look of horror, fear, excruciating pain, great suffering. At the same time there was a peace, a love that I've never seen, a defiant look not to attack her son. She was willing that depression out of me.

That was the turning point. I knew her love for me. From that day I began to heal.

I knew how Mary must have felt as I looked at my own mother. She answered my question. She hugged me as I left. She literally saved my life on that day. The power of that moment was a power I never felt. There was a connection, a bond, a oneness.

— written by a high school student for **Family Memories**

How have I dealt with depression in my life or the life of someone else?

Have I had someone help in my struggles simply by being present with me?

Who has loved me in such a way that I felt a surge of new life come into me?

Do I sense the power of a higher being in my connection with others?

5

RON: This far out in the country, there were no water lines available. For our water supply, we put a cistern underground on the back of the house. This concrete area became our back porch.

Once the house was up, we still had to thoroughly clean all those filthy logs. The wallpaper and clapboard had been mostly removed before it was assembled, but the plaster and nails still had to be cleaned up.

MICHELE: First we had to pull out all the nails that had held the clapboard on the outside. Ron pulled out hundreds of nails. And on the inside, we used wire brushes to get off as much plaster and wallpaper as we could. Also, we had to remove all that mud between the logs.

RON: I cleaned the remaining plaster off with diluted muriatic acid. This was an awful job. I tried not to splash it on myself, and I wore rubber gloves.

MICHELE: Because of the windows and doors in the front, only two logs went the full length of the house, but one of them had a thin spot and had broken. When we found this broken spot, we were worried because these full logs were important for keeping the house together. Roy worked at it and found a way to connect the broken log. We put a little wooden cross on it as a symbol of trust in God to hold the house together. And it held. The cross is still there.

RON: At this point, we had a shell of a house. We had walls, a basement, and a roof, but no plumbing, wiring, or interior walls. None of this was included with the original house plan so we were on our own.

MICHELE: In a house made of solid logs, electric wiring was pretty tricky. We didn't want the wires running up and down the walls. So, they had to drill through the logs and some of those logs were oak. One day we were out there and the electrician was trying to drill through an oak log and he kept breaking these big long drill bits. Finally, he just threw the drill down and walked out. I said, "No, no, no!" Every time something like that happened, I worried whether we were ever going to be finished and actually get to live here. But Ron just patted my back and said, "He'll be back. He'll be back. It's okay."

RON: We would get a little discouraged at times, but we would have faith that this was going to be completed. I had no doubt!

MICHELE: This house was so iffy and I kept saying, "Is this really going to be a home?" When something like this would happen, it felt like it would never work, but Ron kept telling me that it would work out. And he was right. The electrician did come back, and he finished the job despite the challenges.

RON: Aside from the few oak logs, most of the logs were poplar. When we had to cut into them, they were still yellow inside and looked new, despite being from the 1840s. Poplar is extremely resistant to weather and insect damage and the trees grew so tall and straight, which is why the pioneers used them. We had oak, poplar, and a couple of walnut logs, but the original pioneer builders had shaped them all by hand.

MICHELE: There's not a saw mark on them because the original house was built before there were sawmills out here. It was all done by hand. I touch these logs and

wonder about the people they sheltered before they were ours. Each log is special. After 48 years, I know each one. The poplar one over the kitchen sink, the very wide one by the stove, the black walnut one that runs the whole length of the house in the back. Each one unique. Just what we wanted.

RON: The logs were now up and the roof on, electric and plumbing in place, but between the logs was open space. We had to close that up. Again, we didn't know what we were doing, so we asked people. The guy who sold us the logs gave us contacts of people who had rebuilt log houses. They explained how to use plastering mesh, cut pieces the right size, and nail them into the spaces between the logs. Then you put chinking on the mesh, which is made of cement, sand, and lime. This was a delicate process. You had to make sure the chinking didn't come out past the edge of the log, or it could trap water and cause the log to rot. We had to hand mix so much cement and sand and lime. We did make mistakes, not chinking some places correctly. Later those places leaked, and we had to caulk them.

MICHELE: We had friends, especially Mike and Julie, who helped us a lot with building the house. The logs are different shapes and sizes so the spaces in between them are different sizes as well. We measured each space and cut the heavy, hard plasterer's mesh to fit.

RON: We worked on the outside of the house first, nailing the mesh between the logs and spreading the cement mixture over it. Then we pushed in six-inch thick insulation on the inside. This was very tedious, time-consuming work.

The logs are about eight inches thick. That white between the logs is a sandwich. Mesh with cement, insulation, then another layer of mesh and cement. It took us weeks to do this. It was very satisfying to see the house closing up as we worked.

MICHELE: I had so many muscles because Julie and I would mix the cement and carry it to Ron and Mike!

RON: We were doing all this labor ourselves, and learning. But when it came to the fireplace, we had no idea how to build one. We thought this time we would let someone who knew what they were doing build it. We asked Roy if he could build the fireplace with fieldstone from the little creek on our property. He thought about it a moment then said, "I've never done this before, but I watched my father do it. Okay, I'll do it." Michele and I hauled all the rock from the creek in our little Datsun truck.

MICHELE: We made many trips hauling all kinds of rock from the creek in that little truck. But then Roy looked at the pile we had collected and told us some of it would not work. He taught us which kind we could use, and why the other rock would not work. From then on, we knew what he needed and only hauled that kind from the creek.

RON: He built that fireplace so beautifully and so artistically. We were amazed at the craftsmanship. We had never seen a fireplace that nice.

MICHELE: He laid the hearth with the fieldstone, too. He used one big flat stone, about two feet by three feet, which he had gone down to the creek and found himself.

RON: We built the whole house with that Datsun truck! We put stones and rocks in the back, hauled them up, and hauled lumber home, all in that little truck.

It was exciting to see the house all closed in, finally looking like a real house. But there were still no inside walls, only plywood laid down on the first floor, and there were just beams going across for the second floor. We could look up and see the roof from the first floor. The first thing we needed to do was to put flooring on the second-floor beams.

MICHELE: I asked the builder, "Well, how do you do that? What do you do?" And he said, "Well, you put plywood down, then you put either rugs or wood on top of that." I said, "But then when you look at it from underneath, you'll see plywood with nails coming through?" He said, "Yeah, that's right. You have to put something on the ceiling of the first floor to cover that up." But I thought that would be a lot of work. Wasn't there something else we could do?

We started looking at flooring and I spotted some tongue and groove decking that was a beautiful pine and thicker than normal decking, so I said, "Why don't we just put that down? We'll have one layer. Simple and a lot easier! It looks pretty as flooring and from underneath."

Luna Moth, Roy King

El Mercado

With a group of high school students on a mission trip, we spent time in a homeless shelter for men and families. The purpose was to expose the boys to those who struggle, who are homeless, who are poor, in order to have them become more compassionate, caring young men. The group was to always stay inside the shelter with the guests.

As I left them for a time, I instructed them to not go to the marketplace, which was a block away. Of course, as soon as I left, they said among themselves, "He's not going to let us go to a restaurant. Let's go to the market and eat a good meal." And off they went.

As they were eating, sitting beside a large window, they could see the wide brick walkway. On the walkway was lying a man with people walking around him. The students said, "We cannot just sit here. We have to help." Three of them went out and stood around the man, who they could see was injured. People continued to walk around him.

The boys went to a nearby policeman and reported the sight, but he didn't seem to be concerned. They could not just leave the man there. They helped the exhausted man get up and took him to the shelter.

When they arrived, they were told he could not come in at this time. It was closed for entry for the day. The boys replied, "Then we will not come in either." The attendant relented and opened to the young teens and the man. They then took him to a bed and laid the man down. His sock, covered in blood, clung to his foot. They knew the sock had to come off. One of the boys took off the sock and, in spite of the wicked smell, he then washed the poor man's feet.

The next morning, they gave him food. When I was again with them, they excitedly told me the whole story. I then read them the story of The Good Samaritan from the Bible. Listening, they said, "This happened with us!"

Though we were in the third day of our trip, we could have ended the mission right then and there. For they had lived the experience of compassion, care, and the poor. They were changed.

— a friend

Would I do this and help such a man?

How often suffering can be ignored. Why?

What would I say to these boys who have helped this man?

Dignity of the Poor

In the mountains of Appalachia, a missionary told of the wonderful people – the quiet struggle that many endured, the beauty of the children, and the importance of education. These are some of her words:

There was a small boy whose parents had the mental capacity of children. At one point, the father was in prison, so the mother and the newborn boy lived with the missionary and volunteers. They taught and encouraged this intelligent little boy and, thus, he was far ahead of the other students. He would read for his parents and help them to make their grocery list. When he was in grade school, his father asked that the boy spend the night with him in his small home instead of with the missionaries. That night, he was playing on a flood wall and fell down an open gate and died. How this must have affected them all, especially the father, to lose this special child.

Another couple lived in a tobacco barn with one brass bed and a couch. There the mother, on a clean sheet, delivered her baby after a night of labor. The two boys slept on the couch. They owned one cup and so the father would make a cup of coffee for the one missionary, clean the cup, and then serve the other missionary. They were still so generous and kind with little to offer.

On another day, the missionary was walking in nature with a nine-year-old boy who had been in an abusive home. As they walked in the winter surroundings, the nine-year-old spotted a small, green blade of grass. He excitedly said, "Look at this green blade of grass! Isn't nature beautiful?" Even despite all he had been through, he found beauty in such a simple thing.

In their poverty and struggle, you still see the beauty in their souls.

— a friend

Who is truly rich and truly poor?

Do I appreciate the very simple things of life?

How do I feel about poor people?

My Grandfather Flew a Kite

During my younger years, my father criticized me so much that I felt utterly worthless. Once his influence was removed by divorce, I began to recover. The greatest influence in my life was my grandfather on my mom's side. I loved that man more than I'll ever be able to love anyone else. For several years after the divorce, he became my father. We did everything together; flew kites, rode sleds, and watched movies. He was not only my rock, but he was also the cornerstone of my family. Without that man, I wouldn't have had a positive male influence in my life. He was the best father and friend that a boy could ever have, and I feel if God has ever given me a gift, it was those wonderful years I had with my grandfather. He died my freshman year of high school. It hurts to remember his death, but the memories of our good times are a tower of strength to lean on when I am weary.

— written by a high school student for **Family Memories**

Who has supported me when others have let me down? How?

What feelings of struggle did I have in my teen years?

The Illegal Deer Hunter

Late one evening I was on my way home from my job as a game warden when I saw a man spotlighting a deer and shooting it. When a deer is spotlighted, they freeze in place, making them easy targets. This practice is illegal. I stopped and told the man he was under arrest for illegal hunting. There was no reason to waste the deer, so we placed it in the back of his truck.

The man told me his little son was at his house alone, so he wanted to go there to see that he was cared for. I told him I would follow him to his home. I followed him on a dirt road, then a creek road. Finally, there was a little rundown house with a dirt floor and a single light bulb hanging from the ceiling. And there was the son, a little boy about six or seven years old. There was no food in the house. The man had to hunt to provide food for himself and his son. He was also unemployed.

The man said, "I have to take my son to my sister's home. I was wrong to hunt like that."

I said, "Before we go, we need to dress out this deer."

We prepared the deer, and I asked if he had a refrigerator. He had an ice box. We placed the deer there. I told him not to do this again and I went my way, thinking, "Some folks ought not go to jail."

He was a good man. After that he did menial labor and did not violate the law out of friendship and respect.

— Ron Jackson

What would I do if I were the warden?

Do I forgive mistakes in others, and can I forgive myself when I make mistakes?

Do I have compassion for those who struggle?

I Am Moved

A retreat for homeless men. The invitation didn't sound very inviting. After some clarifying questions my image of the experience was more complete, however not more inviting. The men, many of whom had experienced periods of homelessness, would all be coming from recovery houses around town and be somewhere in the first three steps of the 12 Step process. Still not sure why I agreed.

In one of the first sessions of the retreat a man introduced himself; "I'm Tyler. I'm an addict. I'm a liar, a cheat and a thief." (In the succeeding years I would hear this, or something close to it, repeatedly.) This, and all the introductions and exercises to follow began to reveal just who we were working with here. All broken men. All grieving broken relationships, lost possessions, lost jobs, lost careers, lost lovers, lost trust, lost lives. Many having served one or multiple prison terms. This was not the first time Tyler made this confession; he was practiced at stating these truths about himself. It may have been his first retreat, but it was not his first spiritual experience. He was in the process of internalizing the brutal truth that naming your sins – as clearly and directly as possible, then taking full responsibility for them – was the way to healing.

As I sat and listened, my judgmental side began lecturing me: These are exactly the people you've been told to avoid. The irretrievable. The lost. The hopeless and the helpless. And yet...

The day and weekend wore on. My judgmental side, I noticed, wasn't talking as loud. My human side was beginning to sense a bit of awe and wonder. These men were doing something that was taking me by surprise and putting me, most properly, in my place. These men were exhibiting behaviors that not only surprised me but which I envied. Their honesty and openness were humbling. One man told, and wept through, the story of the final days of his son's dying of cancer and him wishing the death would come quickly so that he might get high again. Another told, again through his tears, about being sexually abused as a boy and being lost ever since. An older gentleman, in his sixties, lamented that he must make recovery work this time because he knew there would be no more chances. Instead of being repelled by these men's past behaviors, prison sentences, rap sheets, and general trail of destruction, I found myself developing relationships with them.

They honestly shared their sins and their desire, in the midst of a sinful and flawed existence, for a life of love and relationship. Isn't this our lot in life? All of us?

I realized through their remorse and their sorrow that I was witnessing the sacrament of reconciliation in organic form. They knew their sins for they had been catechized in a wholesome form of examination of conscience through their 12 Step work, and they had a firm purpose of amendment. I was moved from judgment to a realization that these men were children of God.

Recidivism is cruelly high among addicts and alcoholics.

Through my twelve years of going on retreat with these men, it has become clear that the challenge of recovery is daunting. But whether a person recovers or falls back, they remain a child of God. I can deduce that the beauty is also still there when they go out, fall off, use, find themselves back on the street. God doesn't leave them.

— Bill Schlater

What can I learn about the goodness of a person in spite of their weaknesses?

In the midst of my own weakness do I appreciate myself as a gift? As a good human being?

White Dog

I never had a dog of my own, thus when I had land of my own, I planned to search for a pet dog. We had lived on our acres only a few months, when one sunny afternoon I went walking in our field some distance from the house. As I started back to the house there suddenly appeared a mostly white dog with a few brown spots and of average size. He approached me with some hesitation. I said, "Hi, white dog, now go away." I walked on and he began following me back to the house.

The white dog stood outside the back porch as if to say, "I want to live here." I soon said to my family not to feed that white dog as he would stay if we did. Of course they fed him. He remained outside. So, I gave him to a teenage student. However, a few days later, the student returned the white dog to me because the dog barked so much at night. I could find no one who wanted this barking dog with a broken tail.

So, I surrendered and announced to my family, "Okay, I guess we will keep him. He can stay outside, and we will feed that white dog outside with dog food and food scraps." And thus began our life with this dog. We simply called him "White Dog," except when we visited the vet. Then we called him "Prince." The vet told us he was a mixed breed German shepherd and terrier.

For the next 12 years our pet, White Dog, lived outside in warm weather and cold weather – sometimes very cold weather. He seemed to thrive in all temperatures and conditions – from sunny days to rain and snow. He would only come in the house briefly when new people arrived to check on them and us, I suppose.

Our two children would climb on him, and he remained calm and accepting. He would walk with us on the roads and field, ride in the back of our small truck, never a collar on him. He became part of the place.

For some reason he did bark at night in front of the house until we hollered, "White Dog, be quiet!" Always faithful, he would gently watch over my wife and our place. Never did he threaten anyone, always friendly and meek. However, one day he protected me.

As I was working on the car, I suddenly heard loud growling and much movement. I quickly turned and White Dog was fighting with two very large Great Danes, one twice his size. Soon they had him down on the ground and were biting and chewing on him. I yelled, "They are going to kill him!" I ran for the shotgun, came to the front porch, and shot into the air to frighten them away. White Dog broke loose and came running to me. Later, I located the owner of the Great Danes, and he said the larger dog was very dangerous to people and was scheduled to be put down and had broken loose.

Ron Stegman

The two dogs had come up and White Dog sensed the danger to me and had attacked them in order to protect me. He had been willing to sacrifice his very life for me. He had a large open hole in his back from the fight, which did not seem to bother him. I treated it with antibiotics, and he did heal. I said, "White Dog, I love you."

Then, one day, he left as quickly as he had appeared. He began to have trouble on his back legs. I would wheel him over and put him in his very humble doghouse in the evening. One morning, I went out to feed him and White Dog had died during the night. This white dog had been a wonderful gift for 12 years. These many years later I still miss him and feel emotions well up in me when I think of this humble, faithful White Dog.

— Ron Stegman

Has some pet or animal made my life richer?

This dog was willing to die for his keeper. How does that make me feel?

Often, we hear of the heroic deeds of dogs, or we hear of a cat staying close to someone ill. How do I explain this?

Surprised in Teaching

Once, preparing a play to be given by my teenage students, the lead actor became very ill on the day of the play. We were bewildered. How could we present the play? Could we have someone take the role and just read the lines directly from the script or do we cancel the play?

Suddenly, a young man who had a minor role walked up and said, "I can do the part. I know all the lines and every move." What? We could scarcely believe what we were hearing. He went on, "I watched everything, and I know the scenes and the character."

We had a short run through the scenes. He did not miss a line or a movement, and he knew the character. At his performance that night no one suspected that this thespian had just taken on the role that very day. He received a standing ovation.

Another time, I did an improv skit in class with one of the students. He was very thin, and I had been concerned about him. As the skit developed, he soon had the entire class and me laughing. He and I improvised as small children making bubbles in the water. We played off of one another and made it up as we went along. He was so funny and full of vitality. I was surprised at his skill as he had often missed the drama classes. It turned out he had cystic fibrosis.

The following year, one of my students informed me that this boy had died of the disease. I couldn't believe the amount of life he had given to this skit while having this fatal illness. His performance that day and that of the young man have stayed with me these many years. To me, these are two of the outstanding performances I have seen in my life.

— Ron Stegman

A moment in time that stays with you. What special moment do I have in my life?

Have I been surprised by the gifts of some people I had taken for granted?

What talents do I have which are little known by others or hidden?

A New Life

I was an attractive Black woman and moved from a small town where the poor and rich were separated, the Black from the white, yet everyone knew about your family. When I arrived in Cincinnati I met my husband. I was reared to believe that a man was supposed to take care of the woman. Well, that myth got destroyed within the first three years of our marriage. My husband thought that a woman was someone to be used and abused. That did not sit well with me.

I tolerated that for about another three years until I said to myself, "Self, what is wrong with you?" I thought long and hard about what my future would look like should I stay in this marriage. After about four hours of contemplation, I packed my bags and left everything behind. Yes! All I took was certain items of clothing that I liked. Everything else was left. Clothes, furniture, food, everything. You see, when you want or need to change, you do what you have to do. I just did it.

I left without any reservations. I got myself a post office box, called a women's shelter, and that was the new beginning that I truly needed. At the same time something was pulling me, tugging at my heart. I didn't know what that feeling was. It was totally unfamiliar to me. One day I heard a voice say to me, "Come to me." I thought I was crazy until a woman at the shelter told me that that was the voice of God. I started to inquire about God. She then gave me a Bible which I didn't understand at first. She took me under her wing and started to teach me on the word of God. I have to tell you with interpreting the word of God, my life definitely had new meaning. The Lord God started opening doors for me; new true, authentic people started walking into my life. I can say without any doubt that my life is wonderful.

I haven't looked back at all. I have no regrets, I have no offense, and the people that He's brought into my life are very special to me.

— a friend

What changes have I made that empowered and improved my life?

Is a Higher Power or God important to me? Why or why not?

Grandma Lucy's Story

My father was the oldest of six immigrant sons. My grandparents were born and raised in Italy. My grandma, Lucy, was a tiny woman. She was 4'6" on a good day with new shoes, and she never had new shoes. They were poor, humble people. My grandma walked several miles to church every day. She had to cross back and forth across streets frequently, because she was terrified of dogs and wanted to avoid them. (If I were 4'6", I'd be afraid of dogs, too.)

We would go to my grandma's house every Sunday for dinner when I was a kid. I got to see and play with my cousins when we went. We played in the field across the street, which had been a dump, so there was always lots of cool junk to find.

One Sunday, as was my grandma's custom, she called me and my cousin into the house for a treat. The treat was always the same. She would go to the white metal cabinet in her small kitchen, open it, and give us a few vanilla wafer cookies, which were always stale. On this Sunday, when I was 10 or 11, she opened the cabinet and took out a bag of Tootsie Rolls. Tootsie Rolls for God's sake! What was happening here? She gave us each a few, and we went outside. Later on, my cousin and I snuck back into the kitchen and took a few more Tootsie Rolls. We weren't afraid of Grandma, because even by then, we were bigger than she was.

It wasn't long after that Sunday that my mom had major surgery, and she was unable to get around. My grandma walked to our house to help my mom. On the way back home, she crossed the busy street to cut across a field to her house. As she crossed the four-lane road, one car stopped, but the car in the middle lane could not see her because she was so short. She was hit and killed. I remember my dad being called home from work at the factory. I had never seen him cry before. Life at my grandma's house was never, ever the same.

I was overcome with guilt. For many, many years, every time I went to confession, I confessed stealing Tootsie Rolls from my grandma. This sin, this act of childhood silliness, haunted me.

Many years later in my 30s when I was teaching religion to junior high students, it hit me. I had been blinded by my guilt. I had lost sight of my grandma's goodness, love, and friendship. I finally realized what my short, holy grandma Lucy would have done if she had known that my cousin and I had taken those Tootsie Rolls. She would have opened the white metal cabinet and given us more.

Why? Why would she do this? Would she have approved of our actions? I finally understood. It was because she was good, not me. I didn't deserve them or her love. She gave freely because she was the source of that goodness. She was excessive with her love. I had found in my grandma a clear and lasting example of what love is.

— Dan Minelli

Have I lived with guilt that kept me from fully living?

Is there someone in my life who is a true example of selfless love?

A Real Live Chicken

When you own chickens, they are forever amusing with all their funny noises and little personalities. But you also tend to get used to their sounds and forget that other people aren't used to hearing such noises. One day, I had to make a call to my cable provider. It was a perfect day outside, so I had my office door open. At first, you have to navigate the automated system. You say the answers out loud, and the "robot" directs your call. I was having difficulty because all my chickens had gathered around the door having a chit chat. One even jumped on my lap to "talk" for me, letting out some nice loud chicken noises. The robot kept repeating, "I'm sorry, I didn't quite get that…"

Eventually, I was directed to a real person. My chicken stayed on my lap throughout the phone call, being even noisier than usual. After speaking to the woman for a few moments, I said, "I'm sorry about the noise. There is a chicken on my lap."

"No problem. So, your cable account...wait, did you say a chicken was on your lap? Like a chicken chicken? A real live chicken?!"

"Yes, a real live chicken," I replied. "She wanted to say hello."

"Thank goodness it's a chicken!" The woman laughed with relief. "I thought someone was yelling help in the background and you had someone hostage and I was going to have to do something about it! I'm so relieved you don't have someone kidnapped. So...like an actual chicken?"

— Shana Stegman

Life offers us many humorous events! Can I think of a time when life allowed me to break out in great laughter?

Do I have times of simply being able to laugh and take in what is happening?

Can I laugh at myself? About my mistakes? What happens when I am able to do this?

The Chained Puppy

As a child going to and coming home from school I saw a chained puppy, a Dachshund, with no water or food. The puppy was crying out.

In the evening, I told my parents about this puppy. That night, I was awakened by my father telling me he had taken the puppy and had it with him.

My father, a farmer, never allowed animals in the house. That puppy slept with them that night and every night for the next 16 years.

— a friend

What did my father do which has left a lasting impression on me?

When have I seen suffering and been moved to help the situation?

How has love changed me?

6

RON: We bought the decking. It was delivered on Christmas Eve and stacked on the first floor. We were a little hesitant because we had never laid flooring before. We really didn't know what to do. But as usual, every time we needed to know how to do something, we found someone who had that experience and was willing to help us. With this friend's help and Mike and Julie's, we were able to put the whole second floor down in one day. I felt like that was the turning point. It was key to finishing the inside because we could reach the upper walls to chink them, put in a second-floor ceiling, and frame up the walls. This cabin was starting to feel like our home.

MICHELE: The first room we chinked inside was the room we had decided was going to be our bedroom. So, the only place in the whole house that was somewhat finished was that bedroom. And that was enough for us! We couldn't wait any longer. After working on the house for ten months, on March 1, 1976, we moved in.

It was a little rough. Actually, it was a lot rough. The house wasn't closed up well. We could feel the wind blow through the house. There was no furnace; just a small wood-burning stove. There was still so much to do with the flooring not yet laid downstairs and no kitchen cabinets. We also still needed to divide the upstairs into three bedrooms and a bathroom. But we were home! No more driving back and forth from our apartment to work on the house.

Through the entire build, we focused on simplicity. I only fought Ron over one piece of luxury. I wanted a second bathroom. We compromised with a half-bath downstairs.

RON: Once we got the flooring in, we had to do the framing for the rooms upstairs. We had a vague plan. We would measure and say, "Okay, here's a room, frame it. Okay, here's the second room, frame it." Downstairs, except for the little half-bath, we left it all open. We wanted it to feel free and to have room for groups to gather. We put plywood up on the framed walls and used the barn-siding that the contractor had given us to close in part of the hallway upstairs. We bought cedar boards to close in the rooms.

MICHELE: We wanted one more wall of barn siding, but only had scraps left. So, I designed a sun burst with those pieces and Ron put it up above the stairs. For the rest of the hallway, we put plywood up and covered that with a nice material that looked similar to burlap and fit the feeling of the house.

We had to decide what to put in the third room upstairs. It was a smaller room, but we wanted to have three bedrooms. We tried to use everything we already had to keep things simple and not waste any more than we had to. We had some decking left over from the floor, so we turned it sideways and used it for two of the walls. Ron asked, "What are we going to do for the last wall, cedar or burlap? What do you want?" Everyone had their opinions, but I felt that this decision was important. That little room had such a good feeling about it, and I wanted to make sure the design fit. I said, "Let me think about it." I went in the room by myself, got quiet, and thought, What would be good here? Then I felt it. I knew it had to be the cedar. Cedar was stronger and more beautiful. I walked out of the room, and I said, "We need cedar!" And Ron said, "Oh good, that's what I was feeling, too!" At this point the room became special to me, and it has always held a special feeling for both of us since.

Ron wasn't very proficient at nailing and cutting and building. But Mike was very good at it. They had to cut the cedar boards just right to meet those uneven log walls and that wasn't easy. Mike would measure and cut the strip to the exact size he needed and put it up. Meanwhile, Ron was praying like crazy to find the right piece of wood to fit in. He would take the scrap pieces Mike had set aside, and he'd just put them in another spot, and they would fit. Mike said, "I can't believe this! I can't believe it!" because it just kept happening that the leftover part he had cut off was the perfect piece that Ron needed for the area he was working on.

RON: At an auction, we bought 10 doors for $10. They are now the front door, the back door, the basement door, the bathroom door, and we used one to build a work bench in the basement. I made the upstairs doors myself out of cedar and there're still there today. I had never built anything like that before, but I had learned a bit by now and was quite pleased with myself.

One of the logs in the living room area had a round hole all the way through it that some previous owner had apparently run a stovepipe through, and we said, "We need to close that up."

MICHELE: Ron tried to cut a piece of log to go in there, but it was too hard to get something to fit. We tried a lot of different things, but nothing seemed to be the right fit. Finally, we got two small round picture frames that were the right size to go over the hole inside and out to make a clear glass window.

But I wondered, What could we put in there instead of just two pieces of glass? As always, I wanted something interesting, something different. We went to a little flea market, and I saw a piece of stained glass. It was round with a blue bird in it, and we both liked it immediately. We had a lot of bluebirds on the property, and it felt like it was meant for the house. I said, "That will fit the hole exactly!" And it did. We aren't early risers, but if I get downstairs early enough, the morning sun streams through that little stained-glass window, projecting its bright colors into the house. Sometimes, even the moonlight makes it beautiful.

Ender, Shana Stegman

Ender

On a hot July day, my girlfriend and I were floating down the river in our rubber raft to celebrate her birthday. Our dog, Ender, was darting around – to the front to see where we were going and to the back to see where we had been. Sometimes he would just swim along with the boat until he wanted to come back on board. Watching Ender play and enjoy life somehow helped us enjoy it that much more. Often, if our animal is happy, then we are happy.

We were enjoying the ride, letting the boat float on its own, until we saw a bend in the river and prepared to steer. A couple of waves rocked the boat and a few gallons of water washed over the side. We grabbed our paddles and straightened out the boat just as we saw bigger waves bubbling and roiling ahead of us.

Ender positioned himself at the front so he could see the wave and bark at it. We approached the first wave and the boat dipped into it as we paddled hard and straight. Then the next wave, the biggest wave, was ahead of us. Ender moved to the middle of the boat, and I told him to lay down so I could paddle. The water rose up and curled back at us. I thought it would break downstream. Our boat pitched forward, and the water rose well above our heads. The water spun the boat around 180 degrees. The front of the boat dipped down into a black void of sucking, spinning water. Out boat bent at the middle, no match for the strength of the water. I tried to paddle backwards, watching as the whole front had disappeared into the blackness along with my girlfriend.

The river pulled, the boat twisted and filled with water. Still in the boat, Ender began to dog paddle. This seemed strange to me that he was swimming while still in the boat. Down he went, under the waves, and then it was my turn. The raft bent and twisted and pitched me into the river. I tumbled and spun under the powerful, swirling waves.

While I awaited my release, my girlfriend and Ender had already broken through the surface and had swum over to the upturned boat. My girlfriend held her paddle in one hand and the side of the boat with the other. Ender was paddling and clawing at her side looking for her help. She could not keep herself afloat along with Ender and she knew he was a strong swimmer. It was difficult for her, but she released him from her grip. The current was moving them to a place that was even more dangerous. She had to get back into the boat to save any of us.

The wave let me go and I pulled air into my lungs and caught up with my girlfriend. I was surprised that she still had her paddle. I had immediately let mine go. We righted the empty boat and climbed inside. I scanned the shore for a glimpse of Ender. I asked my girlfriend, "Did you see Ender?" She said, "Yes, I saw him climb onto the shore."

I looked around for Ender and whistled for him, but nothing. I asked my girlfriend again, "Are you sure you saw him get out?" She confirmed again that she had. She could tell I only half believed her. My fear and doubts would not let me entirely trust that all would be well. I wanted to see him running toward us, happy and ready for fun. I wanted to see him safe on dry land. My thoughts kept drifting to the dark depths of the river, the undercurrents that drag things down and claim them.

I watched the waves, imagining them spitting his body out. I looked at the steep hill on the other side of the river. At the top was the highway with speeding cars. I began to search the hills, calling Ender's name and whistling as loud as I could. I walked back and forth on the highway many times. I imagined someone seeing him and picking him up, taking him away from me forever. I tried not to panic and continued to search.

Eventually I made my way back to the boat. I saw my girlfriend watching the water in case Ender found his way back to her. My hopes were dashed when I saw her face. I lost a bit of my composure as she put her arms around me. I said, "I can't believe we lost him on your birthday." I didn't know what to do. I didn't want to leave the spot where we had last seen him, but we had been there for three hours. This was my best friend. He was my family, a part of me. He was not a pet; he was an equal. I came up with a new plan; something to hope for. We would float the rest of the stretch of the river to where our van was parked, pack up, and then drive up and down the highway until we spotted him. The last mile of the float was rushed and joyless.

We passed a patch of willows, then the wild sunflowers and the tall grass between the water and where we had parked. I could just see the top of the van sitting in the parking lot, the sun beating down on the roof. We pulled up to the side of the stony shore, jumped out, and pulled the boat out of the river. The feeling of despair had not lessened. We looked at each other, sighed, and then prepared to unload the boat.

Once more I looked up at the van sitting in the middle of the parking lot, miles from where we had started our journey. In the small patch of shade underneath the rear bumper, there was a darker patch that almost looked like a black dog curled up, waiting. I whistled and the dark patch stood up and revealed itself – Ender. He ran toward us, and I wanted to scoop him up and hug him and tell him I was sorry and promised to never lose him again. He got closer and I spread my arms out. "Hey, buddy," I said, kneeling down. He was happy. He was running to us to show his relief after a taxing ordeal. But wait, he had to stop and grab the nearest stick. He picked it up, got close enough to us, dropped the stick at our feet, and crouched in his "ready for action" pose, nose pointed straight at the stick.

There was none of the jumping into my arms, shivering, and face lapping I had expected. There was just his favorite game – throw the stick into the river. I tossed it and watched the stick float in the water as Ender went after it, as happy and carefree as ever.

— Shawn Roberts

The dog teaches us how to live freely. What frees me?

Life is joy, sadness, fear, hope, sorrow, gladness. What life experiences have deeply filled me with one of these?

I Deeply Appreciate You

Mom and Dad,

The past two months we spent together are so precious to me. This was truly a special time. Spending this much time with family is something I think people neglect, especially as they become adults and create separate lives.

This time has given me a chance to get to know you all over again. It has been so many years since we actually spent this many days together – probably not since my mid-20s when I still lived with you. And in my 20s I was in a different (more selfish and obnoxious) mindset. Spending time with you now that I'm an older adult allowed me to absorb it more and focus on our relationships on a deeper level. Although the pandemic has stolen so much from all of us, it also gave us this unique chance to spend this kind of time together. Otherwise, we would have been distracted with other aspects of life – friends, appointments, errands, meetings, etc. This forced us to make one another a priority.

I have been reflecting on many things since you left. You have always been the most invested and interested parents when it comes to my sister's life and mine. Down to every detail, you have a genuine curiosity and care for us. You never intrude in our lives, yet you are always available and want to know us. You are this way with everyone in your life, which is one of the many reasons everyone loves you both so much. My husband also commented on how you always look out for his emotional wellbeing and not just the facts or physical aspects of things.

You both find joy in so many things. Dad was commenting on how he loved the sound of the geese calling as they flew over the lake. I never thought much of that sound and somewhat ignored it. After he said that it really hit me, and I saw the bigger picture. There is so much depth and awe in something I hear almost every day.

I struggle with aging. It's painful for me to watch others age and one of my greatest anxieties is aging myself. But you have helped me see it in new ways as you have aged. You may have some health issues and not always accept it, but I have seen that you both have so much more youth in you than you realize. Your open hearts and minds, your constant wonder in the world, your resilience through hard times, your constant curiosity of everything. At times I feel older than you because I have lost so many of those characteristics. Being around you helps me try to – or at least want to – find them again.

One of the last days you were here, Dad said, "God has guided me my entire life." I jokingly said, "Fear has guided me my entire life." I have been thinking about this a lot since then. Without being sure about a higher power or feeling that anything is leading me, I'm still searching for ways to follow something more hopeful and reliable than fear.

Before you came for these months, I had some fear that I would be too sad seeing you in your aging. I was afraid it would be too difficult if you were struggling or suffering at all. As you are in a new phase of life, so am I in a new phase of my relationship as your daughter. I am able to return some of the help and care you have given me all my life. I found a lot of beauty in that. Feeding those who fed me, giving to those who gave so much to me, helping to walk those who taught me to walk! I feel grateful to be in this stage of life with you.

Throughout my life, you gave me everything I needed – material things, emotional support, advice and guidance. You gave me life and then supported me to turn that life into a whole self, a whole person. And now that I have gone through life, gathering some of my own strength and wisdom and love, I hope I can share with you to return some of these things, to keep each other whole.

You are always 100% your authentic selves and live so honestly and confidently in who you are. You are weird, unique, special, and important. I know without a doubt you both were put on earth with great purpose.

I know you have a lot of change and uncertainty ahead of you. This is a difficult time. I hope I can support you in the ways you need. I guess I don't need to worry so much since apparently you have God leading the way? Not knowing what the changes will bring is scary, but you also have no idea what good may come from this big life shift.

Thank you so much for being here with me for this time. I love you both so much and appreciate all you've done for me in my life.

— Kira King

Who do I need to thank and appreciate in my life?

What have I not shared with family or friends that I need to say?

Does love hurt me at times?

What Handicap?

When I was young, I contracted a disease and was paralyzed from the neck down. If it hadn't been for the many sacrifices that my mother and father, sisters, and other relatives made, I would not be the same person I am today.

My mother and father took me from the hospital to our home, and there they gave me extensive therapy until I was able to walk. One of my sisters, who was a teacher, tutored me through the seventh and eighth grades. My other sister gave me encouragement to get out of bed and lead a normal life.

I think my childhood illness has helped me to appreciate and accept all people the way they are. It has also given me a strong will and the determination to overcome obstacles.

My wife will sometimes do things around the house that I think I should do, but I realize that she is just protecting me from trying to do things I can't. My children have never mentioned my handicaps except in a kidding way. I hope that by my example of never letting anything hinder me from living a full life, my children will be able to cope with whatever problems they may face in their lives.

— written by a friend for **Family Memories**

With loving support this man lives a full life. Who am I supporting to live more fully?

Who has given me an example of living a good life with some type of handicap? How?

Do I accept people the way they are?

The Illegal Immigrant

On the night of July 15th, Josue was crossing the Rio Grande River in an innertube with two other men. The innertube was a tire from a big truck. The people in Mexico helping them cross told them to take off all of their clothes except their underwear. Their dry clothes and shoes were put in plastic bags to carry over their heads. Josue said the women trying to cross were devastated to be nearly naked.

None of the people could swim and it was frightening to be in the black water late at night. The water was deep and moving quickly. They really could not see well but there were ropes guiding the innertubes of migrants from one side of the river to the other. When they reached the other side, they dried themselves as best they could, put their clothes on, and coyotes took them to a warehouse. They lived in the warehouse for 10 days. There was little food and they had to be quiet. There was nothing to pass the time. The people kept hearing they were going to San Antonio. One night, about 15 men were taken out of the warehouse and they were told to get into a waiting pickup truck. Everyone wanted to ride in the cab – it had a backseat. Josue had an uneasy feeling and thought it best to ride in the bed of the truck.

The truck had not gone but a few miles when the Border Patrol stopped them. The coyote was handcuffed, and Josue thought his life was over. His greatest fear was the Border Patrol. But instead of being mistreated, the officers gave the men water, food, and cookies. Josue was so grateful, but he was close to tears, his stomach was in knots, and he could not eat. He was afraid of what was going to happen to them. The Border Patrol took the migrants to San Antonio, but instead of freedom, they were placed in cells for five days. They were then bused back to Mexico, a place called Tamaulipas. Josue lived on the streets and begged for food. After five days, he decided to try a second time and cross into the USA.

A small group gathered at the banks of the Rio Grande. Again, it was a very dark night, and it was frightening. The night was still except for the whisperings of the people wanting to cross and those helping them. They were told to strip down to their underwear and the migrants were given a bag for their meager belongings. The people told them not to bother to dry off when they reached the other side this time – just run, run, and keep running. They were told people were there waiting for them across the river, but if they passed through the town someone would help them. It was terrifying not to know where to go. Josue was put in a huge innertube with another man and a woman. The woman was whimpering. Josue said a few words to try and give her courage and take away some of the fear. The three of them were about halfway across the river when, out of nowhere, the searchlights were upon them. The helicopter was so loud, and the whirring of the blades sounded like they were just a few feet above their heads.

As soon as they reached the bank of the Rio Grande, Josue got out of the innertube and just ran. Hope and fear guided him to run and keep running. The helicopter was now higher, and the spotlight kept going back and forth. He felt he might make it and kept running to find the people that were promised to help.

Ron Stegman

Dogs started barking and he sensed the police after him. Josue heard their pounding footsteps and the shouts to him in English. He had his shoes on and his underwear, but his clothes were still in the bag. Josue was afraid to look back. The footsteps stopped but Josue kept running. He felt so lost. He was out of breath and there were sharp pains in his ankle. Josue saw a car and he crawled underneath it. He scraped his skin and prayed no one would find him. About 15 minutes passed and he heard the police shouting. He saw boots surrounding the car. Josue was caught.

He crawled out and, again, the police were surprisingly kind. They let him dress and gave him water to drink. Josue was taken to El Paso and spent 10 days in the jail there. It was called the "Freezer." The jail cells were so crowded, and the stench was unbearable. Josue was given one of those aluminum blankets athletes use after a race. The only place to sit or sleep was on the concrete floor, or, if you were lucky, a concrete bench. It was very cold. Each cell was packed with 50 people. There was one toilet in each cell.

Every five hours, the prisoners were moved to another cell. It didn't make sense, but that is what they did, all day and all night. The women were in different cells. If the children were under the age of six, they could stay with their mothers. All other children were separated from their mothers and housed separately. If a child was with their father, no matter the age, they were taken away. He did not know where. After the 10 days in El Paso, buses came and took all of the migrants to Monterey, Mexico. Josue never got the chance to fill out papers for asylum. There was nothing...

— a missionary friend

Why do I think people endure such hardships to enter into another country?

What feelings do I have after reading about Josue?

What human conditions in my life made me change or leave a situation or place?

Am I afraid of certain situations?

Sand

My last two years of college were marked by great learning and great unhappiness. I was unsure of what all the reading and reflection were calling me to do with my life, unsure of myself socially, and my way of dealing with all of that was to drink heavily at parties. I was trying to figure out who I was, who I am, all the usual searching of late adolescence and early adulthood swirling and mixing with questions about identity, about the discomfort of living in my own skin. I was in great pain, though I am not sure I knew it while I was going through it.

Graduation came. At the big celebration graduation night, I left the party at 9:00 p.m. and went to bed. I had figured out that drinking was no longer really working for me. My friends must have sensed my building depression. Two friends asked if I wanted to go on a post-graduation adventure.

"Where? I have no money."

After a few ideas they said in unison, "Michigan."

We made plans to leave. We drove to the University of Michigan, Grand Rapids, and then to Lake Huron. We saw Sleeping Bear Dunes on the map and decided to check it out.

We drove into the park. Massive sand dunes faced us. "You can walk all the way to Lake Michigan, but it's a long walk in the sand, boys."

Yeah, but we're men, and we didn't come here to play in the sand. Let's go. We packed nothing. No water, food, sunscreen. The sand was hot. Very hot. We ploughed up the first slope. A straight shot uphill for some forty yards. We pressed on. I was tired immediately. I was in horrible shape and my two friends were college athletes. My drinking binges often ended with a trip to the 24-hour donut shop. My body rebelled with every step on the sand. Why were we torturing ourselves when we could be so much more comfortable in the air-conditioned car with delicious homemade donuts and destinations to explore by driving?

Ron Stegman

We had already trudged a long way when a huge wall of sand greeted us. To get to the lake, we had to go over it.

"Come on, man, let's go," my friends said.

I tried and slid down immediately. I tried again. No good. I looked up. Both friends were nowhere to be seen. Anger began flaring throughout me. I hated all of this.

"God, this sucks. I hate what I'm doing here. Why is my life so bad right now? What did I do to deserve any of this? This is such bullshit." Memories of my life bubbled up within me. Without really noticing it, I was making my way up the sand.

Memories continued, of hurting others, of being hurt. Maybe I had been addressing God through it all, but God was now the brunt of my anger. How could you have let that happen? Why this, why that? Do you care about anything? My most recent painful struggles came up. With everything I had, a voice erupted from deep within me. "Fuck You, God! Fuck You!" With that I flung myself over the top edge and lay down on my back on the top of the sand cliff.

I looked over to my left. My friends were running around the plateau like little kids. I felt the anger still simmering in my guts. What had I just said? What happened here?

An enormous calm came over me. I felt a peace I had never known. I don't usually hear voices, but a voice came. "It is going to be all right. It is going to be all right." It was a most beautiful voice, soothing, peaceful. I cooled and relaxed back into the sand even more, those words salving the pain I had experienced. I let my body be completely supported by the sand. I let go – maybe for the first time.

I felt a surge of energy flowing through me. I began running full blast to the car. My friends didn't know what had gotten into me. I didn't either. I ran as fast as I could, the years of beer and donuts jiggling at my side, feeling freedom and openness within me like I had never known.

Part of me struggles with what I said to God; part of me knows I could have never held back those words – at least not for much longer. I suppose the Creator of the universe can handle someone cussing him out. But I do know this. Without those words like poetry erupting out of my mouth, not much would have happened in my life. What is hidden deep within us must be said, must be told.

Walter Brueggemann, a scripture scholar, often speaks of the words of the prophets as "poetic eruptions," words that pour out of our mouths without any filter, words that come from our depths, our deepest urgings, and longings, our truest speech. As I look at all the tragedy in the past years, all the senseless violence, the greed, those who wonder how they will survive, I wonder from whose mouths the poetry will erupt to call us to what really needs to be said, realized. When will we be transformed together by words?

— Brian Shircliff

Do I hold in some feelings that need to be expressed or spoken?

What obstacles in life keep me from happiness or living fully?

Do I talk with others about my feelings?

Freedom to Be

They ran in rick-rack lines around the yard, clearing the grass of all the crickets and grasshoppers they could scare up. The Guinea fowl weren't ours, but they were daily visitors, running rampant through the neighborhood, little football-shaped vacuums that belonged to someone, somewhere down the road. We loved to watch the loony birds. Not much sense but a lot of comedic entertainment.

One day, they showed up with little miniatures, trailing behind, mimicking the antics of their parents. For days, we enjoyed watching the little babies, bobbing and weaving and learning to survive in the wild. Their vocals were noisy and raucous, often irritating, but too funny to complain about. Sitting on the porch one evening, we were watching this daily show; the birds finally moved on, probably returning to that unknown coop in the unknown yard. A few minutes later, we heard it...a lone little distressed cry, under the cedar tree. We heard it again, but there were no adult Guineas in sight. So, we followed the cry and found a wild-eyed baby Guinea, crying fruitlessly for someone to come take her home. We tried to catch her, but she ran, naturally afraid, and searching frantically for a being that looked like her.

Stupid birds, they are, but we found ourselves developing some complex plan of attack, one in which we could successfully outwit her, nab this little babe, and enable us to keep her safe from the coyotes, the raccoons, the bobcats, and any other predator that enjoys meals of the feathered kind. It was getting dark and apparent that "Ginny Guinea" had been left behind.

Finally, cuddled in our hands, we found a box and a water dish, and I delved into my role as "mom," running in rick-rack lines around the yard, catching every cricket and grasshopper I could. Ginny, too small to swallow them whole, proceeded to beat them unmercifully against the side of her box until they were dead or unconscious enough for her to eat the best way she could.

I felt a little guilty, because I knew I could never catch enough food to sustain her, mainly because I wasn't adept, but also because I had to go to work. The Guineas did not return the next night...they generally foraged during the day. They did not return when we were there, for almost a week.

In the meantime, we had grown attached to the sweet little bird that owed us her life, snuggling with her, feeding her, and enjoying the sweetness of this tender little creature. She was obviously not happy, but she was safe. Every day we placed her in the yard inside a portable fence in a bug-rich area and let her enjoy her natural environment, rather than the box in the garage that had become "home." She heard them before we did...that raucous obnoxious cackling that signaled the return of the flock. Ginny was so excited and began running back and forth along her little fence. The closer they got, the more excited she became. One adult came to the fence with interest, but almost immediately returned to the foraging. I looked at him and he looked at me...do we keep her, or free her...

There was really no question. When the fowl got far enough away that I could release Ginny without scaring them away, I lifted the fence and knew the right decision was made. She ran with everything within her toward the flock, tripping and flapping her wings and crying with what suddenly sounded like a joyous sound. She was now free to be what she was meant to be. At risk to the dangers in the dark, but able to live the life to which she was born. We saw her often, after that, trailing behind, tripping and flapping and trying to keep up. Always last. And it seemed she was a bit smaller than the rest, probably due to the "smart" human who did not know how to care for her like her own mother. We still talk about little Ginny with fond memories of that one moment in time when we knew the happiness of protecting and caring for one of God's precious creatures...and the joy He continues to return to us as payment.

— Roberta Jackson

What person or animal has helped me to feel fulfilled or more aware of my surroundings? What did they do?

Who or what has been my little "Ginny"?

How am I changed from a life experience in the past?

Pain of Divorce

While teaching, I listened to some students speak about the divorce of their parents and about their own life after the divorce. So, I went to a visiting school psychiatrist to ask her about the impact of divorce on their lives and how to respond. As we were talking, I told her that my parents had divorced when I was very young. I also told her that my little sister then went to live with our aunt, my very little brother lived with my father, and I lived with my mother as the oldest. At the same time, my mother had to work for us to live. This all happened when there were much fewer divorces.

The doctor then said to me, "How did you survive? You really had no one as all were out of your life and your mother was trying to survive and work to live. In many ways they were dead for you."

As soon as she said this, I felt a piercing in my chest and knew this to be true. I had never realized this until this moment, and I was 50 years old. She said again, "How did you survive?" The one word that came to me was, "God." I said that I always felt God was there. Perhaps this is how I survived and did not feel so alone.

Still the hurt and emptiness is there to some degree. When I think of that sudden loss, I again feel the emotional pain and urge to cry.

— Ron Stegman

Loss and separation of family is extremely painful. How do we cope with these things in life?

How does a person survive and even become better after a terrible loss in family?

To whom do I talk to when I have emotional pain or loss?

The Swimmer

A Comboni missionary arrived in an African village. It was a hot day and the men in the village asked if he would like to take a swim in the nearby river. He asked if there were crocodiles in the river. The men answered, "Oh, no. There are no crocodiles." He heartily agreed and walked with the men to the water. When they arrived, he began preparing to go into the river, but the other men did not. He asked them, "Are you not going to swim?" They said, "No, but we will sit here on the bank and watch you." He stepped on a rock and then went into the water and swam across to the other side, washed off, and then returned. When he was finished with his swim, he got out of the water, and started back to the village with the men. A good man in the village asked him if he had gone swimming in the river. He told the missionary that the river is very dangerous with many crocodiles. The missionary called the men over and asked them why they wanted him to go into the river with the crocodiles. They answered that they wanted to see if he had a good spirit or a bad spirit. "Since the crocodiles did not harm you, you have a good spirit." The missionary said to the Lord Jesus, "Thank you, Lord, that the crocodiles did not know that I am also a sinner. Because otherwise they would have had good missionary meat for dinner."

> — As told to Ron Stegman by Fr. Filomeno Ceja, a Comboni missionary who serves the very poor in the world.

When do I find it easy to trust?
When do I find it difficult to trust?

The Human Condition

Today I have experienced the pain of the human condition from four stories told to me.

A mother told of the death of her young son's teacher. The teacher had committed suicide and left three young children. Her son didn't know how his teacher died. The mother said this teacher must have had great personal anguish. She said her son may discover how his teacher died and she would have to find a way to explain this to him.

A young wife shared the struggle in life that she and her husband are going through. He is considered illegal and is not allowed to apply for residency for some years. He has worked and paid taxes for several years, yet he cannot receive social security. They fear he will be deported suddenly. They struggle together to return to his native country or to hope for some policy change in the United States. They are in constant turmoil. They also have a small child.

A teacher from China spoke of her struggle to learn this new culture and her challenge as a new teacher in a foreign country. Besides these two challenges, she also deeply misses her family.

Later, I had a friend tell me his 36-year-old niece had died. She had small children, and some will have to live with a distant relative. She apparently died due to a mistake in surgery and the death was sudden.

All of this brought a great sadness to me. I find myself hoping and praying that all of these events and painful experiences will have meaning and resolution in the end. I have to trust in the love of a higher power; that all will be well in the end because everything is returning to the Creator, that love will be the ultimate condition.

— Ron Stegman

Do I think this life has meaning beyond what we see?

How do I deal with pain and suffering in the world and in my own surroundings?

Do I believe in another life after death? What do I think that looks like?

Story of Healing

In a high school class, I had the 20 students lie down on the floor for a period of reflection. Just then, the principal entered the room to observe my teaching. Well, I thought, I am just going to follow my plan and see what happens. The principal sat in the back of the room, arms folded, saying nothing.

I had the students look at slides of nature and people. I instructed them to not just look at the slides but listen to what these pictures were saying to them. I asked them to pay attention to what they felt. At the conclusion, I had them relax and share their experiences. As I ended the class, the principal stood up and walked out without saying a word.

Later, the principal's evaluation was given to me. He wrote, "I do not know how you can give a grade for the class exercise, but I do know that when I came into the class, my ulcer was hurting badly. When I left, it no longer hurt."

— Ron Stegman

Do I give enough attention to what I am feeling?

How does being still and being aware of my surroundings help me to heal? Do I have any examples of this?

Women in My Life

Yesterday I had a realization of the power of the feminine, the gift of women in my life. I began to understand how the various women have shaped me as a man and helped me in life. I also realized the need I had (and have) to be in relationship with a loving woman.

I reflected on a young girl who I had as a first girlfriend when I was 12 or 13. Her goodness touched me even then. Then I had my first love as a 16-year-old with a girl of 15. Her affection and my attraction to her drew me out of myself. I felt a new life within me – someone else mattered and not just me. Then a relationship with another girl when I was in my late teens enabled me to go a little deeper with relationships. I began to learn about sacrifice.

When I was in my mid-20s, I was planning to serve as a celibate for life and found myself attracted and beginning to fall in love with a young woman. Her goodness gave me joy, made me forget about myself, and pointed me more to others.

Later when I was involved in a bad affair and trying to find myself, another young woman caused me to break away from the destructive affair and seek a healthy relationship.

Finally, the gift of a wife. She enabled me to really learn about relationships, how to love with commitment, and she showed me how to give of myself and find the peace that God was calling me to experience. She pulled me away from many compulsions, fears, and false ideas, and taught me how to receive and give.

All of these women have been part of my growth as a person and as a man. I realize I always had great need for personal relationships even though I thought I was called to celibacy. I am grateful to all of these women over the 50 years and, especially, my dear wife who taught me total giving in love. She is the best gift in my life.

— Ron Stegman

What relationships have helped you grow as a person?

How did I become a better person through disappointments or failures in relationships?

What gifts do I have that can help others become better?

7

RON: It wasn't always fun doing all this building. Sometimes we both just got tired of it. One day, I was sitting on the steps to the second floor working on something and having a difficult time. I got so disgusted with doing all of this. The chinking, the floors, the weeks – now months – of work. I threw the hammer down on the steps. I said, "I'm fed up with it. I don't want to do it anymore."

Michele started to cry. She was so worried that I was going to abandon this huge project and we would be living in an apartment forever.

It was at this low point, being so tired of all the work, that I heard within me, "Finish this house! You will have thousands of people visit this place!"

It was the motivation I needed at that moment. I picked up the hammer and continued the work.

And we have had thousands of people visit. Thousands. From the very beginning we were planning to open this house to many. We have had retreats, visitors, groups of all kinds. This house was for more than just us and it was important that I continued to build.

I built a railing for the stairway to the second floor with a little dead tree I found in the woods. I just attached it to the wall by the steps as it was when I found it.

I didn't stain it or sand it down. Over the years we did nothing to that little dead tree except use it, but I guess the oil from our hands over the years has made it smooth and changed the color of it. We had taken this dead tree and transformed it with our touch. On the other hand, if you look at the log walls today, they're the same as when we put them up. No change.

Ron Stegman

Dragonfly, Roy King

Surprised by Faith

When I was in my 40s, and the father of a new baby, I had a physical exam, and they found a spot on my lung. The next day, I had a CAT scan and a surgeon telling me I should do surgery to remove the upper part of the lung to protect me from possible cancer. My father had died of lung cancer in his 40s, so I was in great turmoil as I faced this surgery.

At this time, I was teaching a religion class to a large group of students. They were intelligent, questioning young men who were interested in discovering themselves, thinking about their future, and connecting with prayer and religious themes. As I faced the surgery, with fears of cancer, I came to class in a somber mood. I was not feeling very present with the students. So, at the beginning of class, I told them of my worries and concerns with the surgery and that they were not the cause of my change in attitude.

Almost as one, they began standing up and walked toward me as I sat on my chair near the front of the room. The entire group gathered around me and began placing their hands on my head and shoulders and pressing down on me. Then various students began to pray aloud for my wellbeing and my health.

I could hardly believe what was happening. I was astounded that these teenagers were showing such faith and care. I remained quietly present. When they finished praying over me, they silently returned to their chairs.

Astounded, I told them to have this happen, to have them show me so much care and faith, was almost worth the entire experience of my lung problem and surgery. I said, "How could God not hear such a faith-filled act?" This experience would never leave me.

Later, I learned that other doctors disagreed with the diagnosis, and I never had the surgery. Many years later, it has not affected my health again, but I have always been affected by the actions of that group.

— Ron Stegman

Have I been changed in my life by a group or a person's love?

Have I received care from an unexpected person or even a stranger?

Words of Appreciation and Love

Mom and Dad, I love you both so much it doesn't even make sense!

Even when I'm trying to make one of you feel better about something, you still end up making me feel better. "You're so wise! You're right! You're so sweet! That's good thinking!" etc.

You both always stuck up for me to everyone. Always had my side. No questions asked. Because you trusted me. My emotional wellbeing and comfort were the most important things. Besides your obvious love for me, your trust in me was one of your greatest gifts. I remember you telling me I never had to worry about you going through my private things. Because those things were mine. And they were my decision to share or not share.

The fact that you bought a piece of property and built it from the ground up is the most amazing thing. So many of the trees, you planted. So many of the animals that live there now are descendants of the animals that were there to greet you when you moved in. Your place has been a home to so many creations because of the safe and caring environment. And it's all a part of you. Even though Kira and I moved to other places, it's us branching out and sharing the love to wherever we are. We are spreading your kindness and creating a home.

You weren't just good teachers but good listeners and learners yourself. You never thought you knew everything. You knew you could grow from everyone you met and every experience you had. I always felt so important in every decision you had to make because you made a point to ask my opinion and feelings about it all.

You shared your whole lives and experiences with me. Even in the moments that life was hard for you, or embarrassing, or full of regrets. This made me feel at ease to speak with you about my own life and troubles and future decisions. You respected me and I respected you and your advice. You made me feel like an equal in the house; that my thoughts and cares were just as important as yours.

I think of all the moments I miss from when I was a child. Living with you, going everywhere with you, helping with your errands and tasks, so much playtime. I know if I miss those moments, then I had a great life.

— Shana Stegman

What would I say in a letter to my parents?

What childhood memories helped shape me?

What values have I passed on?

Feeding

A group of teenagers, ages sixteen and seventeen, were on a three-day retreat in Appalachia. Much of the retreat consisted of meeting people and sharing a little of life with them. On one of the encounters, we visited a home for the elderly. At lunchtime we sat and talked with the residence and some of them needed assistance eating.

While talking I heard loud choking from another table and then quiet, then choking again. As I turned, I saw that one of the teenagers was attempting to feed an elderly man. I grew concerned that he might be forcing food on the resident, but an assistant informed me that when the man eats, he can have these choking episodes, but he wants to keep eating. I hurried over to see if the young teen needed help. I could see that, at times, the choking would cause some food to go on the student. I asked, "Do you want me to take over for you?" He replied, "No, I can do this." And he patiently continued to feed that gentleman. I believe the man appreciated and admired the teenager for feeding him. I know I did.

— Ron Stegman

How have I fed the hungry even when it was difficult to do? What would I say to that teenager?

Can I think of a time when someone was patient with me when I was difficult to be around?

Words of a Monk

Love is the highest art and the most difficult. Human love is a reflection of God's love.

The whole world is a sign. God is saying something with spider webs, bird songs, butterflies, and dew drops. Every dew drop is a rainbow.

We pass onto our kids what is in our hearts. We are all mystics.

This life is just a prelude for the real act.

This world needs poets, singers, and artists for signs and symbols.

God is forever talking to us in these ways. This enhances the beauty of life.

The above words are from a man who has lived as a monk for about 60 years.

— remembered by Ron Stegman

Do I feel that someone is speaking to me through things like spider webs, bird songs, butterflies, and dew drops?

Do I see myself as an image of my creator?

Does creation move me to question the purpose of life?

An Interview with a Surgeon

He did not want to be a surgeon. So, when the surgeon began doing rotations in various medical fields, he chose to do surgery first, so that he could have this field out of my way. Guess what? He liked it.

He enjoyed surgery as this directly impacts people. A general practitioner can work with people on an ongoing basis but with surgery one can have an immediate impact on their life. After 29 years of surgery, the surgeon most likes training residents. At present he has 20 residents. One can have a big impact in training other surgeons. They need to have a good role model to show them to be a caring physician.

The surgeon cares about people and likes to work with his hands, and he works hard. He is paid to do something which, actually, he would do for free. He said, "I am very proud when I can steer these physicians in the right direction. Most of this is pure fun."

A surgeon must have strong convictions, struggle, and be a worker bee. A good surgeon must have mechanical aptitude, reasonable memory, common sense, strong endurance, and want to work. The really good ones are those who are highly dedicated and work long hours.

This surgeon is a dedicated man. What do I admire about people with this type of dedication?

To what am I dedicated or what would I like to be more dedicated to doing?

What is challenging in my work? What is enjoyable?

How Strange

My wife and I were waiting in a small airport to board our plane for our return home after a visit to our daughter. She had just left us, and we were sad. We were preparing to board when suddenly the airport alarm sounded and resonated again and again throughout the airport. We said to each other, "What's this?"

Then we heard that a plane had crashed at the beginning of the runway. We waited and heard nothing more except that this had been a small plane. About 30 more minutes and there was an announcement, "The runway is cleared."

Later we spoke with our daughter. She told us the people on the plane were a husband and wife who were attempting an emergency landing. She said, "I was outside the airport walking toward my car when this small plane flew overhead. I heard the sputtering, and I thought the plane was in trouble. Then I heard the alarm in the distance. I have learned that the couple were killed. I think about how strange it is that as they flew over me, they were two living people and a few seconds later they were dead."

— Ron Stegman

How do I cope with the knowledge that a chance event can change everything?

Am I able to embrace the gift of life in more moments than I do now?

The Stray

My mom called to tell me there was a stray cat hanging around outside my parents' home. "I found you the perfect cat," she said. I laughed. I was in no position to take in a cat, although I had always said I wanted one of my own. But I was going through the darkest time in my life. I was too depressed to hold a job and too socially anxious to see friends. I spent most of my time locked inside my small apartment with the blinds closed to the outside world. I was contemplating suicide and didn't need another creature in my life to let down.

A few days later, forgetting about the call from my mom, I went over to my parents' house for dinner. As soon as I walked in, I saw two tiny white ears peeking up at the bottom of the window on the door to their back porch. "Oh, the cat!" I exclaimed. She seemed to hear me and popped her whole head above the window with the loudest MEOW I'd ever heard. She was the most unique looking cat. Pure white with huge green eyes and so much attitude.

"She meows like that day and night," my mom told me. "We don't want to keep her so we can't let her inside, but she seems so sweet."

I got some tuna and took it outside to her. I sat down on a chair on the porch while she lapped it up. She was skinny and dirty. Her white coat had turned a filthy gray. Her ears and nose were sunburned, and all the fur had fallen off in those areas. She was a very tiny cat to begin with, but she was just skin and bones.

After she finished eating, she climbed onto my lap and curled up. She looked up at me with those big green eyes and started purring while I pet her small body. I felt something come over me. This little life was immediately more important than my own. No matter what darkness I felt, no matter how much I struggled in life, being here for this cat in this moment made everything worth it. I could feel how much she appreciated the safety of my lap, the kindness of my hands petting her fur. I felt like she was telling me, "We have each other now."

We sat on the porch like that for eight hours. My parents brought food and water for us both and we ate and drank while sitting together. At the end of the day, I told my parents, "I'm going to take her home just so she doesn't have to stay outside anymore. We can look for an owner or take her to the shelter, but I'll care for her until then." But I knew she was mine and I was hers.

When I took her to the vet, they told me she had problems with her internal organs and needed to be put down right away. I refused, knowing this cat still had much life in her. I fed her special food and gave her medicine every day. I put ointment on her little ears and nose until the sunburn healed and her fur grew back. Meanwhile, she gave me purpose and a reason to live. We spent all of our time curled up together, healing.

She lived for nine more years. When she was dying, I thought I might die with her. Our souls were so entwined I didn't understand how I could exist without her. But as she took her last breath, I promised her, "I will live. You saved my life, and I won't waste it. I will find a way to be happy and see joy in life again. It may take me a while, but I will do it for you. Please move on and let your spirit be free. Don't hang behind for me. I'm okay now."

— a friend

Have I ever felt that my soul was connected to another creature?

What has given me the motivation to persist despite times of overwhelming sadness in life?

Mistakes

When I was young, I thought I should be a perfect person – do nothing wrong, never offend God in the slightest manner. I was taught in school that God would punish me if I sinned. So, I tried to be perfect, to do nothing wrong, not even the slightest thought. I constantly looked inward to discover if I had sinned. Eventually I was obsessed with the thought of having done wrong, of having offended God who was watching me. I was miserable. I had feared that God might catch me in a sin.

As an adult, I still tried to be perfect. Then one day I fell hard with a sin of relationship. I even tried to break up a family. I wanted to love at the expense of others. I began to hurt people and

I justified what I was doing by saying this was love. Now, for some reason, I did not fear God. I let go of the fear.

Eventually I broke from the harmful relationship and moved on in life. I now knew I was not perfect, nor would I ever be. I was a human being who had weaknesses and failures. I now realized that this was the condition of all of us. Yet, the Creator accepts me and loves me in my human mistakes and failures.

My very sins and failures led me to be at peace, accept my human weakness, and embrace and accept the humanity of others.

This poem, shared by a friend and written by a six-year-old girl, has the wisdom that I needed when I was young:

> I wish I never made mistakes
> They always make me feel sad.
> Mistakes scare me like snakes
> Because they make me seem bad.
> My parents said mistakes can be good
> Because they can help you learn.
> Like on the day when I forgot my hood
> And my ears started to burn.

— a friend

Why do we sometimes need to fall to accept our own human weakness and failures?

Did I have an image of God as a child? Has this changed as an adult?

Do I accept the weakness of others and still embrace them?

Peten, Guatemala

Last week I went out to nine Q'eg'ohi Indian villages. The first village I visited is made up of people who had come back from the refugee camps in Mexico after the peace accord.

One man told me how the army had come into the village where he lived with his family in 1981. He was standing with his wife and the army started shooting, killing his wife and one small child. He grabbed the other child and ran into the jungle with the army shooting at him. The same thing was happening to all the families in the village at that time. The survivors made it by walking through the jungle for several days and entering into Mexico where they were put up in camps for almost 10 years. Now they had returned home.

— Ron reflects on a story told to him by a missionary

How do I react when I hear of violence against a group of people?

Do I become pessimistic about humanity when I learn of evil being done in some parts of the world?

Mother's Embrace

A girl was separated from her mother for many years. Her mother was very young and had personal problems and was unable to care for her. She agreed to let the girl live with her father and stepmother. The mother was supposed to be allowed to contact her daughter and she wrote to her, but they never let her receive the letters.

After many years the girl contacted her mother and developed a wonderful relationship even though her mother lived a thousand miles away. Then her mother developed lung cancer. The girl told this story:

"My mother was in her home for her final days. After walking a short distance, she returned to bed to rest. My mother was always concerned about her oxygen being there for her. As she rested, she said, 'I hear my daughter pulling up in the driveway.' Then she pulled the oxygen away, lay back to sleep, and died peacefully.

"At the time of her death, I was sleeping in my home a thousand miles away. I had a dream that my mother came and held me in an embrace. In the morning my stepfather called to tell me of my mother's death. We he told me the time of her death, I realized this was at the same time as the dream about my mother and her embrace."

— Ron reflects on Heather Nardini's story

Are we more connected with those who have died than we realize?

Have I had dreams that spoke to me about my life and the people I love?

Do I talk to those who have died?

An Amazing Man

I want to tell you about a man I really admire. There was a wealthy young man who greatly enjoyed the company of others and dreamt of high adventure. He had hopes of being a knight and doing great things. But after being wounded in battle he had time for reflection on what really mattered in life. After this time, he had a remarkable change. It changed him so much that he denied his wealth and material things and became determined to follow God.

He thought about becoming a simple hermit and giving his life to service and love. So, from dreams of a wealthy knight, he instead became a poor man who loved creation and people. He cared for all life. He spoke to all creation as a gift. He spoke of the sister moon and brother sun. He spoke to animals out of love and respect. He lived with hardly a thing because things didn't matter.

People began to admire him and soon many followers were willing to join him in a life dedicated to love of all creation. He continued to live as a poor man with a heart full of love. He suffered physical afflictions and valued his body even despite all of this.

Near the end of his short life, he wanted to die as simply as possible. He told his followers, "Strip me of clothing." Then he said, "Put me outside in my nakedness," and his followers did not want to. He insisted they put him outside in the mud and rain. He died as a simple, humble man in nature. His name was St. Francis of Assisi.

I have always appreciated him for his simplicity, love of all creatures, and love for God.

— Gary Sabourin

What makes me happy? Really happy?

Why is this man, Francis, so alluring to us?

Mothers

As I walked around the outside of the house I heard a clucking sound. I spotted a hen turkey walking in our back yard with her very small brood hurrying along around and under her. They remained with her as she pecked for food while continually calling to them.

I went to my shed to ready the tractor for mowing and as I removed the cover from the lawn tractor, a mother mouse jumped and ran off. I tossed the large nest that sat on the motor to the ground. On top of the engine was a tiny, newborn mouse. The eyes were still closed, and it had red skin. I scooped the tiny creature onto a piece of flat plastic and placed it on the nest hoping the mother might find the newborn. Then, I caught sight of another newborn lying on the ground next to the nest. So, I placed this one next to the first one.

Very soon, the mother returned and, disregarding danger, ran up and around the tractor searching for the babies, ran throughout the small shed, and finally over to the nest on the ground. She poked her head into the nest and came out with a baby in her mouth and quickly carried the young one off. A short time later, she returned, ran about, and then went to the nest once again. She brought out the other baby in her mouth and again ran off. I was in awe watching this tiny creature care for her young. I felt honored and privileged to witness this event.

— Ron Stegman

What a privilege to witness a mother creature care for her young. What can this event teach me? Would I risk harm to help the helpless?

Do I have a reverence for life around me or do I often take it for granted?

Albert Schweitzer said all life is sacred. How do I respond to this? How do I treat creatures like mice?

Ron Stegman

Worms and Chocolate

I was giving a presentation about arctic foxes at the zoo. As I talked, I tossed the foxes food, which included live mealworms. A young child came up to me and asked what I was feeding them. I held out the wriggling mealworms to show him. He said, "But those are alive!" and ran to his mother crying. He told her the worms were alive and they were being fed to the foxes. "I don't want them to eat those worms."

His mother answered, "Well, that's what they love to eat. You eat chocolate because you love it. Do you not want to eat chocolate anymore?"

"Well," he answered, "don't feed them the worms. Feed them my chocolate."

— Kira King

How can I have some of the thoughts of children in my life now?

What have I lost from childhood that I would like to bring back?

What can children teach you?

8

MICHELE: Finally, the chinking was done, and the sand, cement, and lime were out of the house! I was so tired of all the dust and dirt and mess. Now we could concentrate on getting a real floor downstairs instead of just the plywood.

RON: We saw an ad in the paper that someone was selling a used floor nearby. It was beautiful oak flooring. He had pulled it out of a house in Cincinnati that they had torn down. It was over a hundred years old. We bought it and hauled it over, again using our little truck. It was perfect. It covered the whole downstairs except for the kitchen area. It was beautiful, but we had nothing in the kitchen.

We thought, Well, we could buy some kind of flooring for the rest, but I looked out the window and started praying, "God, show me what I can use on this floor." And suddenly, I realized I was looking at some boards outside. The only mistake our builder made during the entire process was that he had ordered too many of the beams supporting the second floor. I saw those beams lying there by the fence and thought, "There's our floor."

MICHELE: You started bringing them in, lying them down in the kitchen and I said, "What are you doing?!" And you said, "This is our floor! The Spirit just told me!" I couldn't believe it. These dirty, gray planks?

RON: They were 2 x 10's. We put them down and it just worked. There were enough to fit exactly, leaving one tiny space, and that's where the pipes for the sink go. The contractor had ordered perfectly. He just didn't know what he was ordering for.

Knowing that we were still hoping not to go into debt, our friends looked out for us and told us where we could get some free fixtures. The sinks were free, our clawfoot tub was free. We hauled them up and put them in. Free. The house was done, and the total cost of everything including the cistern, septic tank, and house...$21,000. Over a period of time, we had earned the money and paid for it as we went along, so at the end, not a dollar owed. For everything. It was done. Then I said, I want a dog...

Kitty, Shana Stegman

Why I Like Cats

I never had a cat as a pet. I never had the desire to have a one as a pet. I knew next to nothing about the cat world. So, when my daughters wanted to keep a stray black and white kitten that appeared at our home, I was hardly enthusiastic. After their begging, I agreed to keep her, but I explained to them that the kitten was to stay outside and never become a house cat.

Of course, over the following years, Kitty was often brought into the house without my knowledge. Amazingly, she won the heart of everyone who visited our house. She was very accepting and affectionate and thoroughly enjoyed being held. People would remark, "What a sweet, friendly cat she is!"

I realized she was a good cat and really no trouble and I would put out her food. Rarely, if ever, did I hold her. Eventually the girls moved from the house, and I was now responsible for her care.

As she aged, I began letting her into the house when the weather turned cold. People continued to be amazed by her sweet, gentle disposition and her fondness for being held. People who never liked cats were easily won over by her. Still, I did not hold Kitty.

As she grew old, the veterinarian told us that she had kidney problems, as cats often do. Now I began taking special care of her with periodic infusions and special cat food. I began to watch over her daily and care for this very gentle pet cat. As she was under my daily care, I began to fear she would soon die.

Suddenly she took a turn for the worse. Her kidneys were shutting down and she refused to eat. I tried feeding her with a syringe with little success. Then she stopped eating. I picked her up and walked outside with her and showed her where my daughter found her and where she used to walk with us. That night as I sat on our couch, I held her on my lap. And then she did something I will never forget. As I held this little cat who was in her final hours, she pushed her head under my hand to have me pet her. Even in her final hours she was asking for the touch of my hand on her head. She died the next morning while I held her in my arms. I will never forget Kitty. And I really love cats now.

— Ron Stegman

Why do we mourn our loving pets so intensely when they die?

What gifts have animals of varying kinds brought to me?

This little cat taught lessons to many. What special lesson was I taught by watching a creature?

The Amazing Body

As I am now old, I hear that I need to drink more water. Older people do not experience thirst in the same way. I looked up the water needs of my body to understand this in a better way. In my research, I discovered how remarkable the human body is in all its systems.

Water
I often wonder how we live with the multiple activities going on in our bodies, every moment. And to think we are water. The human body is about 62% water, and our remarkable brain is about 75% water. All of our bodily fluids are mostly water and practically all the chemical

reactions in the body take place in water. Without water the body dies in about three days. We are water people. I will try to do better.

Blood

Blood can be a bigger issue when older and I notice how I bleed much easier. This led me to look up blood. Our blood is truly astounding. The blood of an average adult is about seven to nine percent of the body weight and such a person has between 4.25 and 5.28 quarts of blood. This is more astounding – about 25 million red blood cells are produced per second, and about 200 billion daily. From where? Red bone marrow. Moreover, there are some 25 trillion red blood cells in the body and the average life span of a cell is 120 days. The body's entire blood supply is filtered through the kidneys 60 times a day or all the body's blood in 45 minutes. I had no idea.

Muscle

I have also noticed my muscles have weakened and I do not warm up easily. In looking up muscles, more amazing stuff – the physical property of muscle tissue has the ability to contract or shorten. So, food is passed along the digestive tract by rhythmic waves of smooth muscle contraction. The contraction of cardiac muscles pumps blood with incredible force from the heart to all parts of the body. And one of the useful byproducts of muscle contraction is the production of heat, and heat is needed to help maintain a stable body temperature.

Heart

Finally, in old age heart issues are especially of major concern. So, I looked up the heart, the most amazing muscle. The heart is about 5 inches long and 3 ½ inches wide. The left side is thicker because it must supply blood to all part of the body, while the right supplies only the lungs. This little heart muscle beats approximately 100,000 times a day, pumping roughly 8,000 liters of blood. Live to the age of 70 and your heart muscle will beat about 2 ½ billion times. Yet, if the heart is deprived of oxygen longer than about 30 seconds, the muscle cells may stop contracting. How can something so complex work so well and for so many years?

How are we able to live without multiple things not going wrong over most of our years?

I feel blessed to have lived all these years with this body. The body is truly a work of art.

— Ron Stegman

Do I regard my body as a gift or more of a challenge? Do I take it for granted?

What do I think of old age and how the body begins to struggle in all its great efforts?

Do I have a healthy respect for my body? What can I do to show more appreciation for what it does for me?

War

My uncle was a very mild and pleasant man to be around. So, when he told me about his experiences in the second world war, I was very surprised, even shocked.

He told us that one day during WWII he was on a hill in the morning and the surroundings were quiet. As he looked about, he caught sight of a lone German soldier on the opposite hill. The soldier was walking down a path and did not see my uncle. My uncle then raised his rifle and killed the man.

I was somewhat startled and asked, "Why shoot him in those circumstances?"

He replied simply, "He was the enemy."

He described to us another time when he was a prisoner at the Battle of the Bulge. The Germans had waged a strong offensive and they had captured allied soldiers. My uncle and three or four others had been captured and were being held in the basement of a home. There were a similar number of German soldiers guarding them. One German soldier told my uncle, "This is foolish. We cannot win this war."

The German captain appeared and told my uncle, along with the other captives, that they would be shot in the morning. Earlier, the Americans had already seen bodies that apparently had been shot. Hearing this, my uncle and the others began to plot how to escape. There were shovels and a pile of coal in the basement. These would be their weapons.

Suddenly, there were the sounds of shots outside and their guards ran to the basement windows. Quickly the prisoners grabbed the shovels and coal to hit and subdue their captors. He used the knife of one of the German soldiers to stab him. They started up the basement steps. The captain came running down the steps and one of my uncle's companions shot him multiple times. The captain fell and, as they stepped over him, he begged for water.

My uncle told these stories more than once and always I could not believe I was hearing these from this man. The horror of war.

— a friend

Am I surprised at what anger or violent behavior can rise up in me?

How do I feel about war as I read these events?

Have I experienced anything that makes me relate to these soldiers?

What Was the Cure?

I had severe pain both legs down to my ankles. The pain in the back of my legs was so severe that I would have to sit down or bend my upper torso forward to have relief. In a store, I would lean on the cart in order to stand and walk. Also, there was pain in my lower back. After an MRI I was diagnosed with spinal stenosis. Some of my nerves were being impinged or squeezed by the surrounding bone and tissue.

The orthopedic surgeon pointed out the damage in my lower back because of the nerves being compromised. Bone spurs and weak ligaments were visible. He advised surgery to correct these problems and for my ability to walk without pain. This would be a major surgery.

I attempted to avoid surgery if at all possible, and sought out the help of two physical therapists, two osteopathic doctors, and another orthopedic surgeon. The first surgeon had told me I would not solve this problem without surgery. The pain continued.

One therapist had given me several physical exercises and instructed me to continue to do these and notice if there was any improvement in the pain. One osteopath told me I only needed a small amount of space for the nerves to be free. He said, "Walk." This seemed strange as I could scarcely walk for more than 20 or 30 feet. The pain continued.

A good friend sent me an inversion table to use, and I would daily do this exercise. I would release pressure on my back through my head and body going down and my legs and feet being raised to the celling. All pressure would be removed.

I persisted. I continued the physical exercise on my own, took a supplement, prayed, and had two groups pray over me. At first, there was no change. By now, this situation had been going on for over a year and a half. At length, I was about ready to accept the surgery. I could not continue living this way. The second group that prayed for me all said that little by little my physical condition would change.

I began walking daily in a field and, after a short distance, leg pain down the back of both legs would come on me. Still, I kept walking this distance on a daily basis. Gradually, I noticed that I was going a little farther each day. Finally, I was walking about a quarter of a mile before the severe pain moved down my legs. After a little time, I could walk out and back with no pain. The physical problem was reversing. There was still some back pain and sensitivity, but I was free of leg pain. Eventually the back pain also disappeared.

What had happened? Did my determined exercises and seeking alternative help heal me? Did the prayer work as a healing source for my back and nerves? I had improved little by little. Perhaps all of these worked together to heal me.

These experiences took place several years ago. Now I never have pain, though I cut and haul wood, climb ladders, and do all types of activity without a problem. I had been told that I would not recover from this problem, yet I am well. To this very day, people continue to ask me about my back and legs and marvel at what happened.

— Ron Stegman

Have I overcome a difficult situation through determination and effort?
Who or what helped me?

Do I think prayer makes a difference in life? Why or why not?

What am I grateful for in my life? To whom am I grateful?

You Will Never Grow Up

I visited a center for neglected and abused children, ranging in age from one to eighteen. They had been neglected or harmed by one or both parents. As we walked into the play area the director pointed out a young boy, awkward in his movements and playing basketball with 10-year-olds.

The director asked, "How old do you think that boy is?"

I said, "Oh, 11 or 12."

"He is 17 years old, but the boy does not believe he can be normal. For a very long time his foster parents told him that he would never be mature nor be normal. He is convinced this is true."

Years ago, the United Nations issued a declaration on the rights of the child in all parts of the world. In part the declaration says, "The child has the right to grow up with freedom and dignity. The right to have a name and a nationality. The right to have good food, a good place to live, and medical care when needed. The right to have loving persons care for them. The right to an education. The right to be protected against neglect and cruelty. The right not to be made to work when too young. The right to learn to love their neighbors."

— Ron Stegman

Was I ridiculed or made to feel less when I was young? Or was I encouraged to grow as a happy person?

Why do I think some adults persecute, neglect, or abuse children?

Wishing

I love you, Dad, for telling me not to wish my life away. Sometimes I would say I wish something were over or I wish it were summer, and you would tell me not to wish my life away. I think of that a lot. Just today I was wishing it was near the end of January and not the beginning of December so the winter would be nearly over, and I thought of what you said. Then I thought, Look at all I would miss if it were suddenly the end of January! I might miss some cold and snow and misery, but I'd also miss Christmas and my husband's birthday and a lot of other things. So that makes me appreciate life more and enjoy the present moment. Thank you for teaching me not to wish my life away!

— Michele Stegman

Often, we are too focused on what has happened or might happen and miss the present moment. How am I at taking in what is before me now?

"Buddha" means "I am awake." Am I? Do I notice how children seem to live in the "now"? Can they teach me about living?

Death of a Child

A mother reflects:

Having to help my mother navigate her own grief opens old wounds and I revisit places I thought were over for me. I am reminded that this is not the case. For the people in this club, we would have given our life one million times over plus infinity to save our child – but, unfortunately, we weren't given that choice. And so, for the rest of our lives, we have to learn how to live with the pain. A pain that is so excruciating, so much like torture, so unimaginable, there's not even an apt word for it in the English language.

We trip over grief just when we thought we had it contained, figured out, put away, managed. We fall into grief potholes when we least expect it. We become adept at carrying it, stuffing it, hiding it places. It leaks from our eyes when we least expect it. We sob in the shower, the car, on the bathroom floor. We dry our tears, put our masks back on, so we can move and be and live in the world, to the best of our ability.

Grief steals the person we used to be, and we grieve that, too. The person staring back at us in the mirror becomes almost unrecognizable. We wish we could be who we used to be, too. We are broken, but there is no fix for our heartache. We carry it with us, always. Grief exhausts us to the bone. There is no reprieve. No minute, hour, or day off from being a bereaved parent. Once a bereaved parent, always a bereaved parent. There is no going back. Even during happy or joyful moments, the pain and sadness is always there. A permanent undercurrent, a pulse of pain. We learn how to carry it all: the joy, the pain, the love, the sadness. Eventually we become an expert at carrying it all.

The moment our child died is now, yesterday, tomorrow, forever. It is the past, the present, and the future. It was not just one finite horrific moment in time that happened last whenever. It is not just the moment, the hour, the second, the millisecond our life became permanently divided into before and after. You might say, "But they died nine years ago!" Or five years ago, or ten. No. No, they didn't. Our child dies all over again every morning we wake up. And again, every moment they are not here with us—for the rest of our lives.

The truth is this fact is almost impossible to express. How many deaths can one parent endure? For the rest of our lives, we will struggle to accept and understand this fact: our child is dead. And in the incessant replay of our minds our child will keep dying all over again for the rest of our lives. This child loss is never over. It is always happening. Again and again and again. It is now, yesterday, tomorrow, forever. It spans both directions.

There is no end.

I suppose you might think I should have figured it out by now. Pardon me while I laugh. There is no figuring it out. There is only the lesson of learning how to navigate this road map.

— a friend

What intense pain! How do we handle loss in our own lives? Does it feel as this parent describes it?

Do I know someone who struggles with a death in their family? What can I do?

What would I say to this parent?

An Old Dog Learns a New Trick

My husband, daughter, and I took our younger daughter's dog, Ender, for a run at the river. He was delighted to get into the water and loved to chase sticks. He quivered with anticipation waiting for the next toss. He jumped into the fast flowing, icy water, and brought the stick back time after time. He never seemed to tire.

Another couple came along with their dog, Flea, and watched as the dogs greeted each other. But Ender was more intent on getting that stick tossed again. We talked for a bit and found out that both dogs were 11 years old. The woman said, "Our dog has never played with sticks and has never seemed interested in chasing and fetching." Flea was watching Ender, jumping into the water with him, but not trying to get the stick. But Flea did keep watching.

Finally, the man got a stick and tossed it into the water for Flea. Flea went after it, but the current swept it away. Another stick, another toss, and Flea chased after the stick and brought it back to the man. He seemed to enjoy it and the man tossed the stick for Flea while we tossed a stick for Ender. The couple was amazed. So were we. Flea had learned a new trick and a lot of joy from watching Ender. I guess you really can teach an old dog new tricks. Or at least another dog can!

— Michele Stegman

Often animals can surprise us by what they can do. Maybe we underestimate their intelligence and gifts. What surprises have I received from the animal kingdom?

Do I think humans respect animals as much as they deserve? Why or why not?

Do I still mourn the loss of a pet?

Ron Stegman

Animal Behavior

At prayer this morning in a monastery, during the priest's homily with the monks sitting in a semi-circle, a young rabbit came hopping into the sanctuary from a side door. He hopped past some monks on the right, and went straight toward the sanctuary, then turned around and left as he had arrived. I saw a few of the monks smiling. An unusual sight, and beautiful in its way. This little rabbit didn't feel any fear as all was so peaceful. This morning, I loved that creature. The best homily this morning was the rabbit.

— Ron Stegman

The simple things can be beautiful, even inspiring. What is one in my life?

Have I ever experienced a small moment that made a large impact on my event or day?

The Child Is Starving

I was at one of the missions in the mountains of Guatemala and a young mother approached me with her young baby. She said, "Here, you take the baby. He cannot survive with me." She opened her blouse and said, "Look, these are full of milk."

I said, "I can see that."

She said, "But the baby cannot take the milk because of his lip. He has a hare lip. You take him and help him."

I said, "I cannot take him, but I will see if I can find help."

I returned to the city and discovered a doctor from the U.S. who did a corrective surgery for this issue. He would operate on the child. But then I could not find the woman! I announced that there was a doctor who would perform this corrective surgery. Fifteen women showed up with their children for this procedure, but not the young woman I had met. A short time later, she did appear. We prepared to take the baby to the doctor, but we learned that he had returned to the U.S.

However, a surgeon in the U.S. said he would do the surgery and successfully operated on the infant. Now, he is a healthy three-year-old with the help of many good people.

— a missionary friend

Do I have any gifts that can enable children to prosper in my surroundings?

Suffering of children is especially difficult to witness or even hear about. What are my feelings when I see these things?

What was an uplifting event with children that impacted my life and feelings?

Grandpa

My mother, my brother, and I visited my dying grandpa in the hospital. I had just had surgery and had casts on. Because of this I was receiving all the attention from the nurses, visitors, and patients. Then my dying grandpa took my little brother aside and told him, "Don't you worry, boy. One day you'll be the one receiving all the attention." My mother said this was a loving and special gesture for my grandpa to notice my brother and take time to say this to him even though he was dying. I think so, too.

— a student shared in **Family Memories**

This grandpa was a man of awareness and care. Whom do I know who has these qualities?

Have there been times I have overlooked my own suffering to care for another?

9

MICHELE: We moved in March 1, 1976. We had started the house in May 1975. When we first moved in, even after we had filled the gaps with chinking and insulation, this house was not closed up as well as it could've been. When the wind was strong, we'd feel it moving through the house. And when it would rain, water would run down the walls between the logs. I was dismayed, worrying about the furnishings, the floor.

RON: When I saw the water inside, I thought, We're ruined! But Roy said to just caulk it and everything would be fine. And it was.

I would take chalk and mark on the walls where the water was running down and the next day I would go out and caulk. After a long time – years – it would rain, and we wouldn't get water inside the house.

MICHELE: Sometimes, we would be in bed and, suddenly, we would hear this loud "crack!" We asked Roy about it, who was no longer our contractor, but now a friend, and he said, "That's just the sound of your logs settling. They're fine." And they were.

RON: We needed something to cut the grass. We were on the hunt for a small tractor. We knew what we wanted, but could we find it at a price we could afford?

MICHELE: I said, "Well, let's pray." I prayed and said, "God, we need a tractor. And could we have a Jim-Dandy tractor? And could we get it free?"

RON: I said to her, "What?!"

MICHELE: I shrugged. "We might as well ask..." The next day, a friend came out to visit and mentioned how high the grass was. He said we would need something to cut it. Then he said, "I have two tractors and I don't need two. I'll give you one of them!" He brought it to us and, we couldn't believe it, it was a Jim-Dandy tractor just like we had prayed for!

RON: The first winter at the house was difficult. There were blizzards, it was 25 degrees below zero, we ran out of water, we had no wood for the stove, the chainsaw broke, the car wouldn't run. I said, "We can't live like this!" But it was a good lesson. We learned how to survive and thrive.

Everything was a gift, even the hardships. Everything. And I felt we had to share these many gifts with others. This house wasn't ours alone. People started coming to the house. We had hundreds of retreats at the house. Students, faculty, and whole departments from the schools would come. Michele would make the lunch and I would lead the retreat. We would also let people live here when we were gone. Someone even spent their honeymoon here. So many visitors, thousands of people, came just to experience this unusual house.

We would come home sometimes and find notes on the table saying, "We stayed here for the weekend," or, "We came for a day." We never locked the house except at night and we were financially free. The people who came, the retreats – it all seemed to bless the house.

MICHELE: Sometimes, I would start to feel like something was missing, things were going wrong. I would tell Ron we needed another blessing. When is the next retreat?

Actually, the first people who spent the night here were not us. Ron was in

church and heard these people saying they wanted to have a retreat, but they didn't know where to go. Ron told them, "We have a house." They came out and spent the night here even before we had moved in. To me, that was symbolic of what we wanted. That became our mantra. People would need a place to get away, pray, or have a retreat and we would say, "We have a house."

RON: The house was a pure gift. So many people would come here and say, "There's something here. It's a special place. It's holy."

Bunny, Shana Stegman

Snip

Our pet rabbit, Mr. Snip, has helped me to recapture some of my youth. At first light, this simple black rabbit runs from bed to door, circles around, jumps a foot or more into the air, races around and under the bed, again bounces into the air, spinning in a circle as he leaps, lands and races to the door once again. He then again heads for the bed, grunts two or three times and then takes off again with another quick jump and skips into the air. Finally, he circles the entire bed and lands on the blankets. By now I am smiling at this little creature and his joy of a new morning and a fresh day.

— Ron Stegman

What helps to lift my spirits when I am feeling somewhat sad?

Children and animals, especially young ones, can teach us about joy and spontaneity. Who have been my teachers to be spontaneous? How did they teach this to me?

India

Many years ago, I visited India and experienced the lives of people on the streets, villages, and roads. These are pieces of my journal entries from this time:

This is my first day and I see women in saris carrying baskets of dirt on their head while nearby an old man cuts the grass with a hand sickle. Near a large fortress a man plays strange music, and a snake appears from a basket. He charges rupees for this presentation. I learn the average wage at this time is 50 cents a day.

Driving through the villages we see bicycles, animals, people walking along the dusty roads. The drivers blow their horns and weave all about the road.

At a corner stop a very old, bearded man gives water to our driver and offers water to us also. He serves mankind by offering water (*pani*) to passersby.

As we walk along the crowded street many stare at us. But they are very friendly. Because of the heat, people sleep on a wooden bunkbed outside in front of their tiny brick houses. In the early morning, from a second story roof where I slept, I look down on the street below. I see a cart pulled by a camel, a man pushing a cart and calling out his wares, an ox pulling a load of wheat, a thin, young boy sitting on his thatched bed, and a poor woman scraping up cow and camel dung with her hands (to most likely use for fuel).

An uncle visits this morning with a gun and bullets strapped across his chest. This reminds me of the wild west. The temperature is now 110 degrees.

In the marketplace, two beggars with no fingers ask for money. As we sit in a tailor's shop a large assembly of local people watch us from the door.

Back on the roof again, I watch a man take his donkey to the city well. The donkey drinks and then the man and donkey move on with the man sitting in a yoga position.

Across the dusty street, a small boy has a bath with a tin can of water poured over him. He screams with delight. Another boy urinates against the side of a building.

I learn that the main cause of death in preschool children are diseases such as polio, tuberculosis, tetanus, malnutrition, and intestinal diseases.

We continue on our journey and camels pull carts loaded with fodder. Many men ride bicycles, a herd of cows block the road, then a herd of sheep and goats. We sight water buffalo in the pond along with people washing and cleaning clothes.

Traveling with a mobile medical clinic, we see a man with tuberculosis, and older woman with acute malnutrition, and a woman and her child apparently suffering from malaria. Another woman brings a child suffering from malnutrition. She has already lost three children through malnutrition.

A wedding party is passing by and stops and gathers around us. The father invites us to the wedding.

We are seeing life being lived and we are privileged to see the dignity of human beings even when they have so little.

These are images of many years ago. But they have stayed with me and made me appreciate these people and their fortitude and dignity. These experiences changed my life to appreciate what I have and to appreciate human beings who must struggle daily.

— Ron Stegman

What do I appreciate about human beings? What do I find difficult to accept about humanity?

Do I love myself or do I find it to be difficult to accept the way I am?

Life, as seen in this journal, is often a struggle, yet fascinating to be a part of. What are some memorable experiences in my life?

A Daughter's Advice for Her Father

I am so thankful I am able to spend this day with you. This gray, rainy, gloomy winter day where YOU give us something to celebrate!

I know that life has been a struggle for you lately and that you aren't feeling as happy as usual this birthday. That is okay. It is human, it is life, and it is real. As much as we wish all our days could be happy and sunny and bright, that's not the way life works. You know this all too well, but that doesn't mean there aren't things to celebrate even in the darkness.

Your birthday being in the depth of winter, when things are the coldest, darkest, and what can be the hardest time to find joy, is a great example of that. Despite all of those things, you brought life and light into the world by being born and being present for everyone through your many years. Every year we come together to celebrate your life and your presence in the world. This gives us joy when we are all feeling a bit dark and cold.

You have always been a light to everyone you meet. Your family, your friends, your students, even strangers who meet you get to see a glimpse of your bright light. That is a gift and I hope for your birthday we can give a little of that back to you. Now is the time you need to allow yourself to accept light from others. We will give you what we have! When your light feels dim, take a little bit from us and use that to find strength and joy.

I love you on this birthday and always.

— Kira King

Have I experienced a time when a child grew to become my teacher?

How has my family helped me to endure hardships?

What special time did I feel supported by a family member?

Quilting

When I was a child in the Kentucky mountains, winter evenings were spent in front of the fireplace quilting. Grandmother was proud of her quilts and rightly so. The quilting frame hung from the ceiling and in the evening, she would let down the quilt and the women would pull up chairs and help with the quilting.

One evening, Mom and Grandmother let me help. I was about five years old, so I wasn't very adept. But Grandmother gave me a needle and thread and told me where to do my quilting. I doubled my thread, put a big knot in it and started. Even I could tell that my stitches were not as close and even as everyone else's.

But I was helping!

Suddenly, Grandmother looked down and saw what a mess I had made in that square. "Oh, Lordy!" she cried. "Look what this young'un has done to my quilt!" She picked at my stitches for a minute than said. "Well, I can't get it out. I'll just have to leave it in."

I felt terrible and got up. But that became my quilt and I slept under it for many years. And I always wanted "my" corner at the top of the bed so I could see it.

I realized years later that Grandmother could easily have cut those stitches out. She left them in on purpose.

— Michele Stegman

What do I have that reminds me of past relationships?

Mistakes are part of living together. What family mistakes do I now think about as part of my growth as a person?

What relatives did I value as a child and how do I still remember them as special?

Midnight Wonder

At midnight I pushed open the front door and heard the door rubbing against the fresh snow on the porch. As I stepped off the porch, millions of lights greeted me. Sparkling, changing, tiny lights reflected off the fresh snow from the full, bright moon.

I walked down the path and watched these sparkles dance. About 30 feet out, I turned around to face our home and was greeted by an unreal scene. This was a magical land. The moon hung directly above the house, enormous in its whiteness and clarity. Thousands of stars shimmered in the cold night sky. There stood a fairyland log home.

The roof held a foot of fresh snow, the sides were painted white with it, and the base of the house was covered in three-foot drifts. Two windows let out faint light.

I muttered to myself, "Make believe places must really exist for I am looking at one this winter midnight."

Wonder surrounded me in the silence. I loved the source of this beauty.

— Ron Stegman

Name a moment of wonder in life. How did I feel?

What is one of my favorite places that makes me feel inspired? Why?

Do I see the world as a place of wonder and a reflection of a creator? Why or why not?

Snakes

I work with lots of snakes, but I was intimidated by a large snake called the Dumeril's Boa who was about five feet long. I was forced to work with him in the off season at the zoo to keep him socialized and used to being handled. So, every week I had to hold him for just fifteen minutes. I soon realized I had misjudged him, for he was a sweet, calm snake and put all his trust in me when I held him. His tail would wrap around my waist to hold on while he rested his head right near my face and slept. He would put his head on my shoulder and let out a little sigh.

— Kira King

What are some of my fears? Could I challenge these?

What judgement have I held about something or someone which I later discovered was wrong?

How do I deal with what I fear?

The Back Porch

One late morning I sat on the swing in our sunroom and just looked around. Spring was beginning to appear, and new life was peeking through – trees, plants, and grass. I turned my attention to the phlox plants outside the window to my left. The plants were now thick, green and covered with small purple flowers. I noticed two bumblebees visiting the flowers, working from one flower to another gathering nectar. These bees were doing what they were meant to do, doing their part in nature and working diligently for life.

I reflected, almost sadly, that soon these tiny creatures would die. Yet they enthusiastically carried on giving life for themselves and for others. There was beauty before me and some sadness.

I went to the other end of the sunroom and stepped out to do some work and lying on the ground was a small sparrow – dead. I now felt more sadness and grief for this little creature that flew into the glass window.

At dusk I once again went out to the sunroom. Then I heard a beautiful song from a bird, then another bird sang. The various birds sang, changing quickly from one to another. I went to the same window where the little sparrow had fallen and on a high limb by the window a mockingbird sat and continued sing to me and the world the most wonderful sounds – I heard robins, cardinals, and others in his repertoire. Each was beautiful and he seemed to enjoy every note. Here was a mockingbird singing of life and doing what he did so well.

I reflected on my day, in this sunroom and the experience of life and death. They go together.

I thought, All of this has meaning. All of this is going somewhere. This is my hope. If not, all of this is meaningless even in its beauty.

In my hope where there is death, there is also resurrection. This beauty, these songs, must somehow continue. This loss must point to gain. Finally, thank you, flowers, bumblebees, sparrow, mockingbird. You are my teachers.

— Ron Stegman

Einstein said, "God is subtle, but not invisible." Does nature teach me about what he means?

Where have I been filled with a sense of awe? Of a presence beyond the ordinary?

How do humans learn about themselves by observing creation?

Connections

I found a tiny, nearly hairless mouse on my cabin floor. I could see the small little legs and closed eyes on this one-inch creature. As I looked closer, I saw that she was moving her legs when I touched her. Alive still. I placed this small bit of life in some wool and wondered if the mother would return.

Later in the evening I returned and found it still alive. I decided to try to feed her with a formula for such creatures. What really moved me was how this helpless animal opened its mouth for food. My wife and I fed her, and she seemed to grow quiet. Later in the night I returned to see if she was still living. No, the body was motionless. This may seem strange, but this small life deeply touched me as I saw this little body move and search for life. I felt connected with life, with this helpless life.

Later, a friend told me how he had been driving and saw something moving in the road. He stopped the car and walked up to discover a cat that had been hit and was struggling and crying out. He reached out and placed his hand on the dying cat. The cat then became calm and looked at him as if to feel comfort and a sense of oneness. My friend said he felt a connection with the suffering animal. Then the cat died. He placed the cat on the side of the road. He said, "I have never forgotten that look over the years."

Both these stories I believe demonstrate a connection that all life has with each other. That beyond our experience there is a oneness in life, a connection beyond what we understand. I think in some ways I will be in communion with these creatures and all creation. The older I grow, the more I feel this.

— Ron Stegman

Do I feel connected with creatures and all creation? In what way?

Do I believe that in some way all will be one with the Creator? Why or why not?

It's Magic

A bearded man worked his wheel, and he moved a mound of clay as if it were part of his hands. Out of that clay he created round pots which grew to six, eight, twelve inches. The damp clay responded to his every touch. With a slight movement of his hands the clay changed, became thicker or thinner, a small bowl or a tall thin pot.

A small child watched transfixed. She stared at his hands and at the clay between his fingers. She watched the spin of the clay, the pot quickly becoming to 12 inches and then, suddenly, she blurted out, "It's magic!"

G.K. Chesterton wrote, "What was wonderful about childhood is that anything in it was a wonder. It was not merely a world full of miracles, it was a miraculous world."

— Ron Stegman

Do I look at the world, at times, as a child again? Or have I lost this gift?

Do I have a place where I experience the wonder of the world?

Reflection

As we grow older, I find we reflect back on experiences in our life, and some are especially meaningful to us. I began reflecting on a few that were special to me and found there were many. Three of them stood out. Not because they are the most important, but because they suddenly came to me. The first one actually surprised me. It was my graduation from high school. I realized after all these many years, on that day, I felt so free and peaceful. I did not have any appreciation or awareness of this at that point. And I now realize how that day was such a gift of peace to me.

The second one happened more than once but it was always exciting in a sense. When we were out, my wife and I would sometimes go our separate ways. Then we would meet up again and it was somehow very special. We would spot one another from a distance, and we could feel the happiness and love of seeing the other once again. This happened many times throughout our lives together.

The third one was a special gift of nature. I was kayaking on the Snake River, which is near the Teton Mountains in Wyoming. I was out paddling alone in the Oxbow area, which is a large body of water off the river. I was sitting in the kayak in the middle of the water and, suddenly, the entire place was peaceful. The water was basically still. I looked up and there were the Teton Mountains right before me. Then I looked over and there was a fish breaking the water. Then there were ducks calling. And geese calling. I saw a bald eagle. It was so quiet, beautiful, and peaceful. All this surrounded me as I sat in my kayak, feeling small in this moment of nature.

These three memories came back to me, and I realized what beautiful gifts I've had in the simple moments of my life.

— Ron Stegman

What special moment comes to mind in my past?

Is there a person in my past that comes to mind when I read this story?

A Chance Encounter

While shopping with my wife I started a conversation with the sales associate. I told her how I met my wife and that she had decided she wanted to marry me long before I was interested in her. I also remarked how I could have married a young woman with the same name as the clerk's.

The clerk began pouring out her life and challenges. "I work two jobs – 25 hours at the department store and 30 hours at another job. I have to do this work to help my children in college and to turn my life around.

"After 35 years of marriage my part-time minister husband took up with his counselor and, eventually, they were married. I was shocked.

"I married right after high school and now I'll have to start over. I found my security through God and friends. I have no idea what is happening with my former husband. Some days I struggle and then pull myself out of this state and begin again. I want to create this new woman who seeks the truth. I live with my daughter and granddaughter."

From this chance conversation with this woman, I've learned everyone does suffer and I have become more compassionate. Now I do not know where my life is heading but I am open to the journey and continue to seek to be truthful to myself and to life. Everyone carries burdens and suffers, no matter who you are.

— Ron Stegman

How does a person have hope after a tragic event or difficult relationship?

If we were to risk love, what joys and challenges can that bring?

Growing Old

When I was young, and for most of my life, I never wondered what life would be like when I was old. Suddenly I have reached that stage of life. Now there are more physical challenges and also interesting discoveries.

Inside this aged body I still feel young and vibrant. The physical body has gray, thinning hair, more wrinkles and skin changes on my face and body, weaker eyesight and hearing that causes me to ask people to repeat their words. I might have even shrunk an inch or more. My mind is good, but I do find it to be more difficult to memorize. A major problem has been balance issues. I have fallen multiple times and find difficulty doing most tasks.

Once I narrowly escaped death in a fall.

Much I cannot do, which I did easily in the past. I feel caring for my body takes half the day. I still have strength to do work but not as when I was young. And I tire sooner than in the past. My time to prepare for the day takes longer as I must do more care for my body than in the past. Colder temperatures bother me now. I wear more clothes and use a sweater when in the past I did not, and complain when I walk in the cold. For me the heat is not bad.

Letting go of so many things in my life has been an enormous challenge. What was ordinary has become extraordinary. I cannot carry a tray up the steps, I cannot walk easily down the steps, I have difficulty rising from a chair. I slowly walk from one spot to another by grabbing what is next to me.

Of course, death has become more real and often I think about my end, but I approach each day with more intensity. At least I try to! I no longer take my health for granted and thank my body for being so good to me. All my older relatives have died and many my own age and even younger have died. Friends have died and I carry them in my heart.

I find it much easier to cry over events, songs, pain in the world. I have more compassion for creatures and creation and for those who suffer. I actually feel at one with creation.

I want to be present for others, but I have very little concern for what people think of me. At the same time, I find it difficult to be fully present for others as I deal with health issues. This fact is frustrating.

Even in dreams there is a difference. When younger, dreams often were sexual and there were dreams of flying. Now I very seldom fly in a dream and very rarely are there sexual dreams. Many of my dreams deal with past work and my career. Is this part of old age?

I appreciate everything more and wish when younger I had the same appreciation. I regret some things I did not do or say. For example, saying "I love you" more often and giving more compliments and thank yous.

Certainly, I wonder what life will be in death. Life has become more of a mystery to me, and I have fewer answers than I used to have. God has become a greater mystery to me, yet more real. At present I have come to believe, to trust, that all life returns to the Creator in an amazing, joyful way.

Eric Hoffer wrote, "To grow old is to grow common. Old age equalizes — we are aware that what is happening to us has happened to untold numbers from the beginning of time."

— Ron Stegman

What do I think about as I watch older people? Do I see any advantages to growing old?

Do I fear death? Do I ever think about being older?

What am I now taking for granted that I might miss later as I age?

Violence

One country has attacked another without U.N. approval. Both nations will suffer, but this other nation will be devastated with multiple weapons. Why must nations solve their problems with war? War seems to bring more violence. Perhaps we will be targeted in the future, our young people will be injured or killed or suffer terrible emotional and mental issues. There will be more repercussions.

People will be killed who are trying to live out their daily lives. Children will suffer and die who do not even know what is happening. I think when we create violence the violence comes down on both the victim and the perpetrator. Perhaps if enough speak up, challenge, question, or call for alternate solutions, the violence will end. Christ said we perish by the sword. War destroys the soul, and, so history shows, destroys a nation. Those who suffer the most are the poor; be they soldiers or civilians.

— Ron Stegman

Do I think the main outcome of war is suffering? If not, what do I believe it is?

What happens inside me when I become angry and strike out at someone?

Love Letters

I never had much problem expressing my love and affection for my husband, but I had a hard time saying anything negative. Sometimes, little things would build up and I would find myself nitpicking. I hated it. He hated it.

One winter day when we were snowed in, we decided to do a private marriage encounter. He went upstairs to write a letter to me and I sat at the kitchen table to write one to him. A few minutes later, he came bouncing down with his letter. I said, "I'm not finished." I'm a writer, and I had found my medium! I wrote him a letter, all right. I wrote thirteen pages.

We read each other's letters. His was wonderful and affirming. Mine, not so much. He said, "We need to talk." And talk we did! I cried a lot, finally having let out so much I had held in for so long. We hugged and things were so much better.

But things began building up again for me and I still could not voice any negative feelings to him. So I wrote him another letter. I said a lot of positive things, because, believe me, there were a lot of positive things to say. But I also wrote the things that were bothering me.

When he came home that night, I greeted him with the letter. Again, he read it, and then we talked. For a long time, that was how I was able to express my hurts and anger until finally, I was able to just tell him the things I was feeling.

Now, we still write each other letters, letters of affirmation and love. Sometimes I leave a small note on his pillow for him to find. Sometimes, he leaves one for me. But the best ones, the longest are for special days, Christmas, birthdays, when one of us has done something special for the other, or just...anytime. We both look forward to those letters. They are not just a way to express how much we mean to each other, but a tangible gift we can keep and reread and treasure.

— Michele Stegman

How do you communicate your negative feelings to others?

How do you communicate you positive feelings to others?

I Stand Before You

In my classes the students shared openly with each other their journey in life and their relationships. Thus, at the end of the school year, each member of my Senior class would give some type of symbolic gift to the class. The gift could be a song, poem, a reading, art, some words, etc.

On the final day, near the end of the class, one of the students walked to the front and said, "I have been truthful to you. I have been honest and revealed myself to you. I have not been afraid to be 'naked' before you." Then he removed his shoes and socks, his shirt and pants. He stood there in his bathing suit. I was thinking, What is this? What is happening here? What if someone outside the door sees this? Then he stood before us in only his bathing trunks and said calmly, "I stand before you as one who has been open to you, as one who has told you who I am. Let this symbol speak."

The class was not shocked. They knew what he was saying. They had been so open with one another and trusting. They could be their true, naked selves without fear. As the teacher, I was nervous at the time, but saw this as a powerful symbol of our truth and honesty with one another.

— a teacher friend

Do I often wear a mask or pretense when I am with others?

Do I think some will not like me if I show them who I am?

Do I fear talking about my feelings openly?

Poor?

When I was a young child, I ended up living alone with my mother after some family issues. We lived in a tiny apartment with just a bedroom and a small kitchen. We lived there for a short time and then moved into a little house owned by a relative. I think we lived there a couple years before we found ourselves once again looking for a place to live. We even looked at a storefront as an option. We lived with relatives for a time where I slept on a cot. We moved in with a woman and her children and shared their apartment. We moved into the upstairs of someone's home.

In about seven years, I lived in five different places. Finally, we bought a house. All this time, we had no vehicle. We would take the bus. Later in life, I thought about this. At the time, I didn't think I was living any differently than anyone else. I just figured this was life, this is how you live! We had decent food and life was simple. Reflecting on it now, I wonder, were we poor, or not?

— a friend

What does it mean to be poor?

Have I ever looked back on a time in my life and seen the experience in a new way?

Dreaming

When I was 19, I had a reoccurring dream. Sometimes it would come almost as a waking vision. I would find myself rising up out of a conical hill. There was a ring of stone and a ring of really old trees around that. When I looked down below me, there was a lake. In the center of the lake there was a forest covered island. There were four streams flowing into the lake but none flowing out. On the Eastern shore, sometimes there was what looked like a small, medieval village with thatched cottages. Sometimes there was a castle there. Sometimes it was almost like a modern camp event with brightly colored tents around.

When I would emerge, I always knew what I had to do.

Sometimes it was to walk down to the village or to find someone I hadn't seen for a long time and needed to connect with.

Sometimes I would dive into the lake and swim out to the island.

Sometimes it was just forest. Sometimes there was a little round house where an old woman lived. She had a boat to get back and forth to get across the lake. She would direct me. She would tell me to find the caves under the water and to swim to the caves.

Often swimming into the caves, it was like going through a door and I would be someplace else.

This dream continued for about seven years. Each time, the dream was similar but also unique. Always the conical hill, with the ring of stones and trees and the village. Sometimes I would have the dream or like a vision a couple times a month or once a year.

I went to visit a friend who lived in Ireland. His girlfriend played the harp and drum. They took us out to a mountain and to some early dry stone stacked homes that were over 4,000 years old. We sat inside one of the huts and she began to sing and play the drum. Instantly, I came to that same place I had been dreaming about.

Afterwards we talked about our experiences, and I told her my dream. She said, "Why don't we go there tomorrow?"

The next day, we packed a lunch, drove about an hour and a half to Lough Gur. This is the second oldest human site in Ireland. We hiked to the top of the conical hill and there it was. The only difference was that the stones were more buried and moss covered, and there was no ring of trees. There was an archeological reproduction of the village and there was the castle. I asked the docent in the village what happened to the ring of trees. She said they had been cut down in the 1920's.

After that, I would have dreams, and call my friend's girlfriend and she would say, "Come on over, and we'll go there." And I would. I have visited five or six places that I dreamed about. The last one I dreamed about, she didn't know where it was. But we found it in a tour book and visited it.

It has, in a sense, rearranged my understanding of time. It's easy to track this linear trip through our lives. But what about ancestral memories or parallel lives? I could be seeing into another person's life in another time or place. It liberated me from my belief that I am trapped in time. I am not limited in terms of physical energy or financial resources but have connections with the universe. If I am not separating from other people or other aspects of creation, there is a living exchange of life and experience. We are not isolated. I am only alone if I separate myself from others and from God.

In the summer of 2011, I was presenting a couple of papers at an international conference on ecological restoration in Merida, Mexico. There was a gentleman there who created geo-spacial models, a type of map. He was working with the villages to protect the forest in Guatemala. He invited me to come to connect with the people, the forest, and do biological inventories. I went and took my climbing and caving and back country gear. I fell in love with the pristine ancient forest filled with some of the most unique creatures. A whole world of wonder. Endangered species, trees whose trunks were 20 feet across and 200 feet tall. The people were like the forest, very quiet until it was time to communicate.

The forest called me in. I spent two weeks there. I was looking at ferns and mosses but also into the canopy and into caves. Cloud forests are known for epiphytes, plants that get their moisture from the air. I was lying on a branch looking at the mountains, the forest, hearing the spider monkeys, the big cats. I felt like I could feel the sap moving through the trees and almost like it was also running through me. And I thought then that I would do anything I could to protect this forest. The prayer that I made there, I said yes, I knew it was not going to be an easy task, but I asked God to give me a sign that He wanted me to do this.

Three days later I was riding in a *publico*, a colorful bus. I had all my stuff on the seat beside me. I looked over and there was a girl of about 12. Maybe she had never seen a white, green-eyed person, but for 45 minutes, she just stared at me, quietly, as if her eyes were the gateways to the forest. I knew that I needed to protect that forest. Over the next four years I brought about seventy people there and helped them also fall in love with that forest. I was able to raise over six million dollars to save and protect this forest. It is now on its way to becoming a new national park in Guatemala, Department of Quiche.

— Jeremy Schewe

Dreams can reveal things about us and the world. Do I have a dream that reoccurs? What might this dream be telling me?

Does my imagination help me live a creative life?

Do I believe a higher power uses dreams to speak to us?

Almost Dead

My wife and I were driving home from our vacation and had been on the road for many hours. Darkness now surrounded us as we drove the interstate. Around midnight the interstate became one lane because of heavy construction with cement barriers on both sides of the lane. I pulled off for a quick rest stop.

As we exited the rest stop, I began to speed up to enter onto the one lane highway. As usual I planned to drive onto the entry lane and then over to the interstate lane. For some unknown reason I suddenly decided to brake before entering. Just then a truck pulling a large boat raced by. It was then I realized that there was no entry lane, only the highway itself. If I had continued for another second or two, we would have been hit by the speeding truck and probably been killed.

Here was a two second interval between life and death. What caused me to stop? I am not sure.

How fragile, often, is the wall between life and death.

— Ron Stegman

Do I think how precious life is even when I am having many issues or feeling bad about my life?

Do I believe there is a presence within me that helps me make decisions?

What has happened in my life that changed me?

Does Prayer Work?

A letter to my friends:

I want to thank you for your prayers, cards, words. You worked God's grace.

In March I was taken to the ICU at the hospital. I was in terrible pain and near death. I was out of my head for three days and was saying, "Let me die!" After testing, I was given a very strong antibiotic, and the meds began to work. I had a severe blood infection. I had a vague sense of being anointed but was basically disconnected from the world.

I did not pray at all. But you did. Two people told me that when they entered my room in the ICU, even with all the activity going on, there was still a peace there – the peace of grace. After three days, when I was more alert, I received a wonderful grace of freedom and I said, "Take me, God, I am ready to die." I felt totally free. Never had I felt such freedom. I was not praying, but the grace was freely given through prayers – your prayers.

Then I had an enormous hunger for communion. When it was brought to me, I wanted to reach out and grab Christ. This and the following receptions of it were the best in my life. I did not pray. The grace of God for this was simply given to me through your prayers.

So, I wanted to thank you for praying. I now understand the gift of prayer and grace freely given. I have health issues still, but these experiences and your prayers are wonderful gifts.

— Ron Stegman (written April 2024)

What do I think? Does prayer work?

Have things happened in my life that are unable to be explained?

10

MICHELE: We tried to live simply. We tried to raise as much of our own food as we could. We canned food from the garden. I had a "solar dryer," meaning I hung the clothes on a line outside. It would have been so nice to have a real dryer so many times, but I thought, okay, try to save the environment a little bit. We just did what we could to live as simply as possible.

RON: That first year I felt uncomfortable living so remotely. I kept thinking about moving back to the city. Michele, on the other hand, was perfectly content.

But my surroundings, the nature, and the house were so peaceful, I changed my mind. This was the real world, not the city. The house with its history, the logs shaped by pioneer hands and now ours, the stone fireplace with all the fossils in it, the wild animals we saw each day, the quiet and peace of the woods.

Anytime we went into town, I couldn't wait to get back to that peace.

We always had a calmness around us. I grew to appreciate nature much more. I experienced life and death around us. All those years there was always a peace about it.

Later, we had two daughters who grew up appreciating the gift of nature and reverence for life. Every day we appreciated the gift of this place, the house and its surroundings. There were challenges to living this way, but we were willing to accept them.

Because we lived simply, we were able to share more with others. One of the most effective things I did as a teacher was a presentation about our house and telling the students how God built the house. We walked in the faith that anything we needed would come, and it did. I shared this story with thousands of people over the years and now will continue to do so with this book. To this day, our house remains a gift, and many of the stories in this book were told to us here.

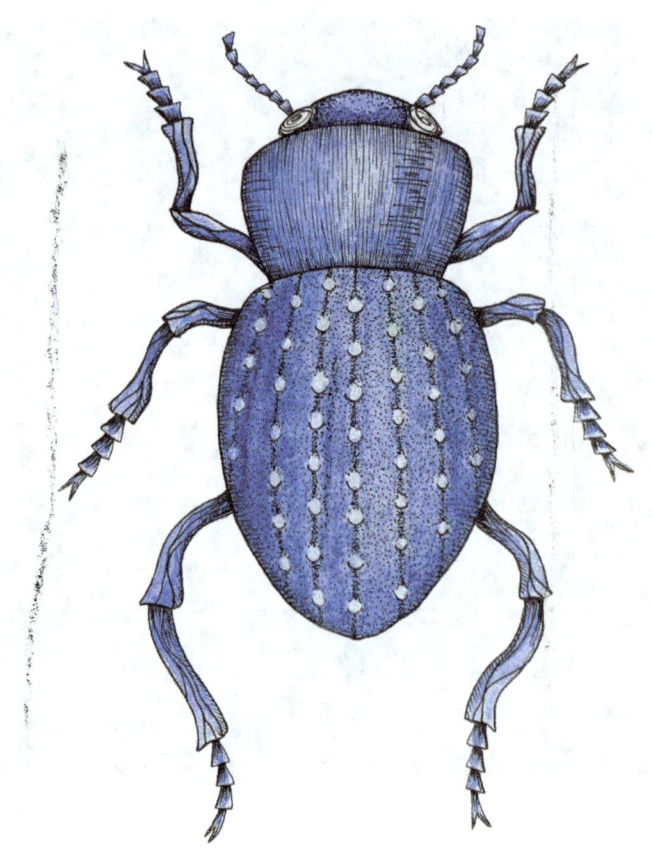

Beetle, Roy King

Kids at the Zoo

As someone who takes animals out to meet the public at the zoo, I have a lot of interesting and funny encounters with kids.

I was holding a blue tongued skink (an Australian lizard), when a little girl asked, "How old is she?"

I answered, "Thirteen."

The little girl became really excited and said, "Now she can go to PG13 movies all by herself!"

As I was showing a snake at our zoo's Halloween event, a little boy said, "That snake is trying to hide in your pocket. He must be afraid of my Halloween costume."

I said, "I bet that's it!"

And he said, "Snakes. Snakes rock."

I was working outdoors at our Galapagos tortoise exhibit on an extremely hot day. There was no shade there and I had to be in the sun for hours to work with the tortoises. A child came up and asked, "Do the tortoises ever go in the water?"

"They go in when they need to cool down."

The child looked at me and asked sincerely, "Where do you go when you need to cool down?"

There is a section of the zoo where you can go into an enclosure with the goats to pet them and interact with them. A little girl around twelve years old came to me and said, "Excuse me, Ma'am, how do you make animals like you?" I told her to be kind, speak to them, and pet them gently.

The girl began petting the goats. I heard her say to the goat she was petting, "Do you know where you are? You are in a zoo. You are here because everyone wants to come and see you and learn about you. Thank you for being here."

Then she came up to me and said, "I think I made a friend."

A little girl touched the back of a little blue beetle I was holding. She would start to walk away, then return and touch the beetle again. She did this three or four times. Finally, as she prepared to leave, she brought her fingers to her lips and then touched the beetle, a loving kiss.

— Kira King

The innocence of children is a joy to behold. What do children do that inspires me to engage with life?

Love of creatures seems to be so easy for the young. Do I still find a high regard for animals within myself?

Did I have pets when I was young? What did they do for me?

How have animals helped me to be a better person?

Meow

Yesterday morning I had an unusual event. This was early in the morning, and I was half-awake. Suddenly, I heard a "meow" just like Kitty, my cat who had recently died and who was very gentle and sweet. The call seemed to be near the bedroom door. I looked at the foot of the bed and our other cat was asleep. How unusual.

Was I receiving some message? A sign? Was the Creator giving me a response to a wish to know about animals in the afterlife? In reading my letters from others who had lost their pets I had read similar experiences and hoped I would receive communication from my cat.

Then I had a dream about Kitty which was unusual. I found myself in a room and I seemed to be standing on a ladder looking down. I saw Kitty walking around the room and she had little wings, which were fitting for her.

I had been asking for a sign from God and, it seemed, I received the messages I craved. Am I a person with a vivid imagination or are these real experiences?

— Ron Stegman

How do I feel about animals living in another life?

Do all things live again?

What are ways the Creator might speak to us?

My Valentine

You asked me what my relationship with God is. Well, I thought about this, and I think my relationship with God is through you. In some way I think that I love you more than God, but in loving you, I love the God in you and see God's love reflected in you. God called you to life so in loving you, I love God.

In loving you God has become more lovable and I can see the goodness of God reflected through you. The heart to my heart, the body to my body, the service given and received – are gifts that give me life and God.

How often I think of our first date and relish that time and know God was calling me to you, giving me the wonderful gift of you. In some way I see most of my earlier years were a preparation to meet and marry you. Graces were given to me to love you and share so many Valentines with you.

Thank you for being such a lovely Valentine, wife. Such a loving woman, such a sweet mother. Always you make marriage an outstanding gift.

I am grateful for your presence, dedication, words, support, love – constant love. I loved you many years ago, I love you more now. This day of love, I want you to know you are my Sweet Valentine and source of God and love.

— Ron Stegman

What are important aspects in a good marriage?

Is there a particular couple I admire who have displayed how a relationship can flourish?

What gifts do you have that help others in their journey?

My Two Regrets

In my early travels there are two incidents that have haunted me over the years. The first one took place in a city in India. My wife and I saw many people sleeping and living on the streets, but one stands out to me. Toward dusk we were walking back to our small hotel when I noticed a very thin Indian woman exit from her cardboard home with her two small children of perhaps five or six years of age. This cardboard house was located right next to the street. I realized, at once, that they had to be barely surviving for her to have two small children and be a woman in India. I thought if I even gave them a hundred dollars this could have a real impact on their lives. I had no money with me and said to myself that I would go to my hotel to retrieve some money and return to give it to her. After I arrived at the hotel, I did not want to leave in the dark, so I did not go out to help her. I have never forgotten this missed opportunity to do something for this very needy family.

The second incident took place a few years later in Haiti. We were only visiting the city for one day and I bought various souvenirs and some simple art pieces in the markets. I had spent my cash. As we prepared to leave a small older Haitian man approached me and asked to shine my shoes. I told him I had no money to pay him for the shoeshine. At first, he did not believe me. I kept insisting I had no money. He finally realized I did not and then said to me, "I will shine your shoes and the next time you are here you can pay me." I paused and then said, "No, I cannot pay you," and I left.

Later, I thought about what I had done and what I should have done. Why had I not handed him one of the souvenirs so he could later sell it instead of holding onto everything I had? Once again, I had missed the opportunity to serve and help someone so humble and so deserving. These two events continue to visit me as I live my life.

— Ron Stegman

What are some regrets I have in life that have stayed with me? An ordinary life presents many opportunities to give love. Do I take advantage of these opportunities?

Who has given me help when they saw I was struggling? What did that mean to me?

Proud Parents

When I published my first book, *Fortune's Mistress*, I remember how proud of me you were, Dad. You would go to the bookstore and hang around in the romance section and when you saw a woman looking for a book, you would hand her mine and tell her it was a good one and that your daughter wrote it. I wonder how many of my books you sold like that!

One day a woman bought a copy you handed her and when you told her I lived far away, she asked you to autograph it! You were so proud!

— Michele Stegman

What person am I proud of? Do I tell them enough?

Do I rejoice in the success of others?

The Protective Doe

As I prepared to step outside, I glanced out my kitchen window to see if the birds were still taking the seeds I had placed on a tree stump earlier on this cold day. Snow covered everything. Then I spotted two deer slowly walking toward the bird seed. One was a doe and the second was her young offspring who was about two-thirds the size of her mother, born in the spring.

The doe walked to the seeds scattered on the ground. The young one stayed back watching her mother. Slowly she approached and began to eat some bird seed. Soon the mother moved back and watched as her offspring ate the seeds.

Then two other deer walked toward them to enjoy this seed meal.

The doe turned toward them and chased them away. Her youngster continued searching for seeds. She slowly began to walk away and soon the youngster followed.

— Ron Stegman

This story shows a mother's love and care. Who cared for me when I was young? Who failed to protect me?

Did I have a friend, teacher, or stranger help me when I was in need or suffering? What did they do? Did I tell them of my appreciation?

Questions for a God

As I become older, it is very interesting how I think of a higher power and about life. In my earlier years, I was much more at ease with the existence of a god and that all is in God's hands. However, now, I wonder more about life, about existence, about God. I have few answers and less certitudes. To me much is now a mystery about this life, this universe.

Why is there such an abundance of suffering and pain in creation? How are You personally involved with each of us within this vast universe? What are we when we go to You? What happens to all the creatures? What does this mean to be in heaven? What if this life is all there is? Why do we create an image of You as being so petty and ready to place us in everlasting misery? So much mystery.

I have had experiences where You have been present and yet I seem to forget these when I come to these questions.

In some ways, I feel closer to You and life when I live with more questions. I have to trust the mystery that You are and embrace the questions as part of the journey.

— Ron Stegman

What do I think about the purpose of life?

When does the experience of living make me confused?

Do I ever experience the presence of something beyond what I can explain? What am I going through during these times where a higher being feels close to me?

The Young Couple

I just learned of a young couple with three children under the age of four who were living on the street. They had been put out of their apartment and had only a plastic bag of belongings. They tried a shelter but were told they applied too late. Finally, a donor volunteered to support them in a rented hotel for six months and supplement some of their needs. Neither of them had graduated from high school as they left their families at a young age. The mother's parents were addicts and she had left to try to make a better life for herself.

The young father was working at a car wash for $8.50 an hour. The St. Vincent de Paul was coordinating their housing and hoped to find them an apartment and job training experience.

How do you help people like this? What do you do? Do you keep holding their hand or let them go? What happens to their children? I don't have an answer to any of this. They were never given a chance to learn how to do everyday things. It makes me feel sad to think of people who are not equipped to handle the basic needs of life when many of us have so much.

— a friend

Do I have compassion for those who struggle just to meet their daily needs?

What are some challenges in my own life?

Why Do I Want to Live?

At times in my life, there seemed to be little reason why I should not want to die except a little uncertainty about the hereafter. Right now, there are many reasons to want to live. The thought, the other day, of dying and leaving you and the children seemed terrible to me. I want to be with you some more, make love, do things together, go places. I want to share in our daughters' lives, give them guidance, love, care, values, dreams, support, encouragement. I want to see them grow and unfold, to see them do all the crazy, wonderful things that life is all about. Dating, school, marriage, children. I want to see the joy on their faces when they hold their newborn children. I want to hold those children, spoil them, and send them home to keep somebody else awake. I want to put my hand on our daughters' tummies and feel new life growing there and share the wonderful feelings they will have.

Sometimes I think I'd like to go back and do it all over again. Through our children is our only chance to relive all those wonderful times we have had. But I also want to enjoy the now. So many things I want to do better for them, for you, for me. I want to go on living so I can write. I want to experience spring again and again. I want to see future space exploration, new types of computers, save the rain forest, end hunger and war, see new miracles in medicine. I want to visit the moon or Mars or some other planet. I hope I'm not too old when it all becomes possible.

I also want to experience the full range of life. What is it like to turn 50, then 60? What will my outlook be then? What new insights and wisdom will I have gained? I hope I'll still be young when I'm 90. There have been times when I felt 90 and I didn't like it.

I want to always be able to enjoy life and nature, to never tire of new and old experiences, to continue seeing things afresh. I want to always have a twinkle inside whether it shows in my eyes or not. I want to enjoy being around younger people. They are so great, so exciting. It's fun to remember and relive the dating years and the school years through listening to and watching them.

Ron Stegman

Just writing this all down gets me excited about life. I want to go out and do it, live it, dance, fish, run, hug kids, experience other's lives, be surrounded by the people who mean so much to me.

— Michele Stegman

This passage is packed with life and the desire for living it. How does this make me feel about my own life?

Do I take life for granted and miss opportunities to be alive to my surroundings? If so, what would help me to change?

What has helped me to feel fully alive in the past?

Message Received

A young man writes on messaging:

If I think about it, I can trace the insecurities I still have back to some of the messages I received as a child. For example, my parents were continually telling me that I was lazy. Like most kids, I would do anything I could to get out of doing chores. They chose to deal with this by telling me I was lazy and thereby "guilting" me into working. To this day I still have trouble relaxing when I know there is any kind of work to be done. But what is even worse, I tend to blame everything bad that happens to me or my family on the fact that I am lazy.

The crazy thing is they gave me so many positive messages and memories. I will never forget my mother telling me I could be anything I wanted in life. She must have said that a thousand times to me. I think those words have given me a lot of self-confidence and really given me strength when I needed it most. And there was never any doubt that my parents loved me, and that love was the most important thing in life. They used to tell us that no matter what happened and no matter how much trouble we were in, we could always confide in them, and they would always be there for us. I will tell you that there have been many times in my adult life that they have proven those were more than just words.

I guess the point is we really do remember the messages we receive as children. The positive ones give us strength and help us grow. The negative ones cause us to have feelings of doubt and low self-esteem. The more positive ones you have, the more prepared you will be to face the demands of adult life. The more negative ones you have, the more difficult it will be.

— a young man

Who gave me hope and encouragement when I was young?

What words have stayed with me for years?

The Faithful Cherry Tree

Forty-five years ago, I planted a semi-dwarf cherry tree. The first few years there were only some white cherry flowers. Then, one year, the tree bloomed full of the beautiful white flowers followed by a multitude of cherries. There were birds feasting on the cherries and I collected as many pints as possible. Year after year, the tree would be covered with the flowers and the cherries.

After some years, there were not quite as many cherries, but it still produced. As the tree aged, growth on the bark became prevalent and some of the branches broke off and died. But the tree continued to produce an abundance of flowers and cherries. Large splits developed among the large branches but still the flowers, still the cherries.

The following year, one of the main branches cracked away and was barely hanging on. Still the broken branches managed to produce the flowers and cherries. Not as many, but they were there.

I thought after 40 years the tree was done, but I still propped up the two main branches. Sure enough, that spring, even the propped-up branches produced some flowers and cherries. As I looked at the tree, it seemed to reflect my own body as I had physical health conditions that were developing.

Now with scales, fungus, rot, and broken branches, I figured the tree would be dead. But, again, in the tree's terrible condition there were still some flowers and cherries here and there.

This spring I do not know if the tree will be alive and give a few flowers and cherries. This fruit tree has given and given for 45 years. But I do know this is a noble tree with dignity even though covered in scales and fungus with broken limbs cracked wide open. It is a teacher to me as in my old age I, too, am broken, laden with health issues, yet also know of my own dignity and ability to blossom still.

— Ron Stegman

What have I learned about myself from nature?

Do I have a favorite place in nature or a setting that gives me quiet, peace, and reflection?

Do I see the creator reflected in nature? How?

afterword

I hope many of these stories and questions were meaningful to you, and perhaps inspired you. Hopefully, this book helped you to be more attentive to life and to reflect on your own life and experiences so that you can record your own stories and ask your own questions.

You are a gift, a story.

acknowledgements

Kira King, our daughter, is the editor of this book. She worked many hours to improve the writing, the arrangement, the clarity of the book. I am so grateful for her gifts and for making this book of life more appealing and readable.

Michele Stegman is an integral part of this book. She typed many of the stories, at times editing them. She wrote, with me, the entire story of the house.

Roy King, Shana Stegman, Michele Stegman: Their creativity and art added to the stories and in a way, each piece of art is a story in itself.

Those who shared their stories made the book possible and bring gifts to others.

Brian Shircliff, the publisher. When Brian heard that I had collected these stories, he immediately asked to publish them, suggesting additions and changes that made the book better. He walked us through each step of this book, encouraged us, and guided us.

Ron Stegman

about the author

Ron Stegman began his teaching career in Cincinnati Public Schools at Gamble Junior High School, where he taught English, Latin, and Drama. After taking a year off, he returned to teaching at St. Xavier High School, where he would spend the rest of his career. Ron taught Relationships, Morality, and Social Justice, in addition to heading up the school's Mission Collection, which gathered millions of dollars for mission projects in India, Nepal, Mexico, Peru, and other countries. Ron also took students on mission trips to Mexico and the Rio Grande Valley. Teaching was a joy to Ron, and after retirement he continued to work with the school by creating and organizing Christian Life Communities, where faculty and staff shared their lives and prayed together in small groups.

Ron always wanted to learn more about the struggles of people in developing countries. He and his wife Michele traveled to many countries, including a two-month trip to India and Nepal, and a trip across Central America.

Ron and Michele have been married for over 50 years and have two adult daughters, Kira and Shana.

Ron has a Master of Divinity from St. Paul Seminary and a Master of Guidance and Counseling from Xavier University. His previous books include *Family Memories* and *Families*.

about the artists

Shana Stegman

Beginning with a BA in Fabric Design, Shana Stegman continued to study multiple art mediums to experiment with different types of art application. She specializes in acrylic, watercolor, pastel and other various crafting techniques. She is thrilled being an art teacher, Artist Representative, Art Therapy Practitioner, and major art supporter. Through sharing her knowledge, guidance, and creativity, Shana encourages others to expand on their individual style and artistic expression and welcomes everyone to see with a more artistic view; she believes that's when one truly sees the world!

Roy King

Roy King III is an ink and watercolor artist who illustrates insects, arachnids, flowers, and landscapes. He is inspired by the symmetry as well as randomness found within nature. He lives in the mountains of Asheville, NC with his wife, Kira, and cats, Avett and Freddie Purrcury.

Michele Stegman

Michele Stegman is a prize-winning artist who works in watercolor and oil. She contributed her painting to this book's front cover. Although she has painted still lifes and landscapes, her main interest is in oil portraiture. She has also published several romance novels, some of which are available at Amazon and other on-line stores. She lives with her husband, Ron.

Julie Lucas

Julie is a graphic designer with Within Wonder who often collaborates with VITALITY. She helped restore many of the photographs in this book taken from Ron and Michele's 50 year old slides which he shared often in his classes over the years.

about VITALITY

VITALITY is a circle of friends welcoming all, awakening each other, and reminding each other that we are Whole. Our affordable self-care programs invite everyone to move, to breathe, to rest, to contemplate, to grow...wherever each person begins their self-care journey, wherever and however they want to become.

It's the power of a circle!

We invite you to explore with us through our

donation-based classes...in person & via Zoom
affordable trainings
individual sessions
volunteer opportunities

vitalitycincinnati.org

VITALITY
buzz, bliss + books

publishing books from VITALITY's circle of friends
inspiring love, creativity, + possibility

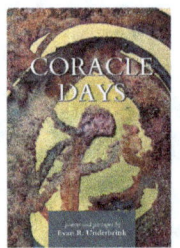

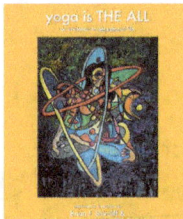

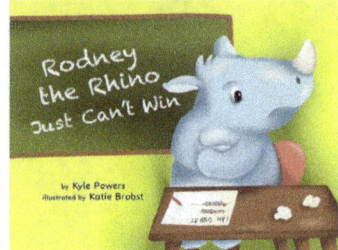

vitalitybuzz.org